Maths Book for 9-10 Y

JUNGLE
PUBLISHING

Introduction: How to use this book

This is a maths book for 9 - 10 year olds based on the National Curriculum in England (Year 5). It also can be used by those in Year 4 wanting to get ahead and by those in Year 6 wanting to cement their knowledge.

The book is divided up into seven parts: Number and Place Value; Addition and Subtraction; Multiplication and Division; Fractions; Measurement; Geometry and Statistics as per the curriculum for Y5/ KS2.

Where you see the ⏱ symbol, this indicates a time trial and you should aim to complete the page you are on as quicky as possible. A guideline time will be given in seconds underneath the clock. Whilst the time trials should add fun it is important to remember that quality and understanding still remain the most important factors.

A marking/scoring system is provided on each page to help measure progress. In addition to this, please use the progress chart on page 4 and 5 to help reflect on what parts of the book came more or less naturally.

Answers are included at the back.

Good luck!

This book belongs to:

Poppy

Table of Contents

Progress Chart

Shade in the star when you've completed a section. For each section, jot down the questions that you found easy and those you found more difficult.

Section 1 - Number and Place Value

Completed ?	What did I find easy?	What did I find difficult?
★		

Section 2 - Addition and Subtraction

Completed ?	What did I find easy?	What did I find difficult?
☆		

Section 3 - Multiplication

Completed ?	What did I find easy?	What did I find difficult?
☆		

Section 4 - Fractions

Completed ?	What did I find easy?	What did I find difficult?
☆		

Section 5 - Measurement

Completed ?	What did I find easy?	What did I find difficult?
☆		

Section 6 - Geometry

Completed ?	What did I find easy?	What did I find difficult?
☆		

Section 7 - Statistics

Completed ?	What did I find easy?	What did I find difficult?
☆		

Determine the place value of the underlined digit. For example: '3 ones' or '6 tens'. The first one has been done for you.

1) 531,2<u>3</u>4 = __3 tens__

2) 507,<u>9</u>31 = 9 hundres

3) 745,26<u>4</u> = 4 one's

4) 80<u>8</u>,624 = 8 bhoush

5) 528,<u>5</u>14 = 5 hundrest

6) 3<u>4</u>2,905 = 4 ten thous

7) 73<u>0</u>,035 = 0 thounds

8) 5<u>2</u>0,291 = ten thous

9) <u>9</u>48,055 = 9 millon

10) 565,<u>9</u>11 = 9 hunden

(9)

Fill in the missing bricks to complete the patterns.

1) | -65 | | -77 | | -89 |

2) | 410 | 426 | | | 474 |

3) | -183 | | | | -207 |

(3)

Score:

1

Add the four numbers to the correct places on each line.

217, 267, 187, 167

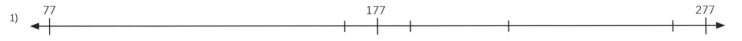

-517, -557, -507, -587

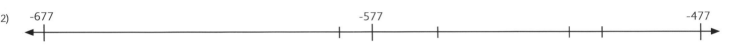

5,092, 5,062, 5,112, 5,012

This time try without the guides.

5,327, 5,437, 5,337, 5,457

-8,890, -8,980, -8,940, -8,860

Score:

Add that which comes either before, after or between those provided.

1) 5,058 __5,059__

2) _____ -5,333 _____

3) _____ -1,164

4) 686 _____

5) _____ -9,031

6) _____ 9,162

7) _____ -3,019 _____

8) _____ 511 _____

9) -5,713 _____

10) -1,743 _____

□
(9)

Round to the underlined digit. The first one is done for you.

1) 2$\underline{7}$2,649 = __270,000__

2) 2$\underline{2}$3,839 = _____

3) 8$\underline{0}$5,429 = _____

4) 202,2$\underline{4}$4 = _____

5) 667,$\underline{5}$93 = _____

6) 300,$\underline{6}$47 = _____

7) 880,4$\underline{8}$2 = _____

8) 588,9$\underline{7}$5 = _____

□
(7)

Score:

Ordering Numbers

Order these numbers from smallest to largest: the first one has been done.

1)
94.43   <u>8.33</u>
8.33   <u>62.73</u>
97.96   <u>94.43</u>
62.73   <u>97.96</u>
8,917   <u>8,917</u>

2)
33.65 _____
68.19 _____
594 _____
16.71 _____
55.69 _____

3)
43.82 _____
2.07 _____
5,364 _____
2,156 _____
3.35 _____

4)
449 _____
8.79 _____
848.2 _____
25.32 _____
68.4 _____

5)
29.4 _____
11.55 _____
8.16 _____
193.3 _____
7,360 _____

6)
371 _____
23.84 _____
5.23 _____
2,509 _____
4.41 _____

7)
758 _____
709 _____
25.85 _____
94.2 _____
578.1 _____

8)
7,164 _____
869.3 _____
62.6 _____
29.00 _____
7,726 _____

9)
79.35 _____
49.8 _____
797.0 _____
1.08 _____
477 _____

Score:

Circle the smallest number in each group.

60s

1)	2)	3)	4)
438.50	46,621.8	53,272.2	62,281
795,264	476,308	6,278.74	1,380.51
943,525	1,059.6	5,414.57	91,674
3,681.95	321,013	581,403	5,900.27
18,740.9	4,322.47	7,702.07	28,179.3

5)	6)	7)	8)
7,699.07	5,815.07	97,301.5	93,757.3
864,687	685,741	79,182.3	2,790.29
95,026.7	32,897.3	65,235.9	80,850.3
54,010.8	54,486.4	24,522.7	741,247
89,497.2	8,150.56	987,589	1,073.10

(8)

Circle the largest number in each group.

1)	2)	3)	4)
76,319.4	1,857.67	708,851	179,162
10,141.4	2,888.28	6,850.76	8,449.96
6,252.51	345,693	962,538	40,341.7
12,371.2	683,577	95,555.7	473,223
818,919	1,499.0	172,007	6,059.01

5)	6)	7)	8)
78,047.7	74,089.8	7,832.51	668,492
147,334	9,755.14	32,954.8	23,943.6
465,732	2,962.29	35,042.6	826,554
50,595.6	593,814	48,271.7	721,188
459,231	83,263.3	5,185.99	7,092.04

(8)

Time: :

5

Score:

Circle the smallest and biggest number in each group.

120s

1)
(2,404)
(401)
874
1,386
474

2)
(426)
728
1,528
(3,738)
2,147

3)
1,821
3,483
(4,615)
(1,104)
4,437

4)
(3,772)
1,426
(83)
88
1,548

5)
4,168
(4,238)
(1,840)
2,340
3,049

6)
(4,567)
3,194
(1,394)
3,816
3,669

7)
3,027
2,633
(3,798)
2,588
(1,470)

8)
(735)
(3,253)
2,343
901
1,812

(8)

This time try with negative numbers.

1)
-9,155
(3,883)
-3,458
(-2,883)
3,614

2)
-6,860
-7,262
(-9,312)
(-1,974)
-8,612

3)
(-6,151)
-3,325
(-1,680)
-4,723
-4,057

4)
-2,398
(2,134)
3,760
-6,747
-4,452

5)
2,259
1,803
4,240
2,029
-5,907

6)
-5,763
1,865
-1,427
3,163
-4,068

7)
973
-7,258
-4,535
-6,708
-7,832

8)
-2,996
-2,102
-8,930
-8,813
-6,227

(8)

Time: :

6

Score:

Fill in the missing numbers. Hint: There is a pattern for each line of boxes.

1)

-10	0	10	20	30	40	50	60	70	80

1)

							700	800	

1)

		-120					-170		

1)

					8,370	8,379			

(4)

Fill in the table, counting by -15 from 80 to -505.

1)   Count by -15 from 80 to -505

80				20					
-70	-85			-130		-160		-190	
	-235								
								-490	-505

(30)

Score:

7

Notation

Write these numbers as words.

1) 311,008 _____

2) 758,999 _____

3) 810,446 _____

4) 88,824 _____

5) 790,188 _____

Write these words as numbers.

☐

(5)

1) _____ nine thousand two hundred **and** sixty-seven

2) _____ eighty-seven thousand five hundred **and** sixty-two

3) _____ thirty-three thousand five hundred **and** thirty-five

4) _____ thirteen thousand five hundred **and** forty-three

☐

5) _____ thirty-two thousand six hundred **and** ninety

(5)

Score:

The Romans used the following letters for numbers.

I	V	X	L	C	D	M
1	5	10	50	100	500	1000

Letters are combined to make numbers, written in order from largest to smallest.

Examples: 7 = VII; 25 = XV; 321 = CCCXXI

However, when more than three identical symbols are required, the number is written as a subtraction instead. Numbers involving 4, 9, 40, 90, 400 and 900 are written as subtractions with the subtracted number written before the larger number.

Examples: 9 = IX (10 -1) ; 42 XLII (50-10) +2 ; 90 = XC (100-10) ; 99 XCIX = (100-10) + (10 – 1);

400 = CD (500-100) ; 452 = CDLII (500-100) + (50 + 2) ; 900 = CM (1000-100)

Convert the values from numbers to Roman Numerals and vice versa.

1) 58 = _____

2) 59 = _____

3) 8 = _____

4) XLIX = _____

5) 2 = _____

6) IX = _____

7) 34 = _____

8) LXIV = _____

9) 6 = _____

10) XVI = _____

11) IV = _____

12) 74 = _____

Score:

Convert these Roman Numerals to years and vice versa.

1) MDCCLXII = _____

2) 1518 = _____

3) MDCCIII = _____

4) MDCLXIV = _____

5) 2003 = _____

6) MDCCCXXII = _____

7) MDCCXCIV = _____

8) MCMLXX = _____

9) 1634 = _____

10) 1811 = _____

11) MDCCCXCIX = _____

12) MMV = _____

13) MDCCCII = _____

14) 1675 = _____

15) MDCCII = _____

(15)

Write the answer to these calculations in Roman Numerals.

1) | XV | + | X | = _____

2) | III | + | VI | = _____

3) | CX | + | VI | = _____

4) | MM | + | V | = _____

(4)

Score:

Work out the relationship between the inputs and outputs and fill in the blanks.
The first one has been done.

1)

Input	Output
163	335
57	229
131	303
104	276

Add 172

2)

Input	Output
144	168
90	114
179	
74	

3)

Input	Output
130	246
53	169
32	
39	

4)

Input	Output
156	350
163	357
76	
15	

5)

Input	Output
153	176
23	46
156	
151	

6)

Input	Output
89	203
114	228
189	
195	

7)

Input	Output
109	110
99	100
133	
56	

8)

Input	Output
95	285
151	341
115	
132	

9)

Input	Output
93	267
65	239
184	
187	

Score:

Addition Puzzles

Solve these across-down problems.

1)

39	+	29	+	74	=
+		+		+	+
82	+	14	+	61	=
+		+		+	+
73	+	78	+	90	=
=		=		=	=
	+		+		=

2)

92	+	90	+	85	=
+		+		+	+
57	+	5	+	61	=
+		+		+	+
100	+	86	+	4	=
=		=		=	=
	+		+		=

Complete these addition tables, some cells have already been filled in to help you.

1)

+	22	14	52	26	97
834				860	
657					754
340					
225					
588					

2)

+	775	550	500	325	19
22					
15					
39				364	
500					
30			530		

Score:

Add these 2 digit numbers.

1)   56
   + 19

2)   60
   + 39

3)   81
   + 60

4)   21
   + 17

5)   62
   + 99

6)   12
   + 84

7)   49
   + 85

8)   77
   + 77

9)   41
   + 42

10)   95
   + 87

11)   89
   + 58

12)   23
   + 26

13)   33
   + 91

14)   85
   + 59

15)   89
   + 80

16)   27
   + 59

17)   54
   + 41

18)   50
   + 65

19)   43
   + 97

20)   62
   + 36

21)   80
   + 14

22)   64
   + 16

23)   19
   + 56

24)   62
   + 98

25)   65
   + 54

26)   42
   + 73

27)   40
   + 82

28)   55
   + 97

29)   95
   + 44

30)   16
   + 89

Score:

Addition 0-100

Add these 2 digit numbers.

1) 74
  + 62

2) 26
  + 81

3) 81
  + 52

4) 40
  + 18

5) 45
  + 21

6) 44
  + 43

7) 79
  + 69

8) 17
  + 85

9) 93
  + 17

10) 17
  + 77

11) 39
  + 86

12) 92
  + 46

13) 48
  + 53

14) 29
  + 71

15) 84
  + 52

16) 70
  + 98

17) 91
  + 72

18) 62
  + 28

19) 86
  + 82

20) 33
  + 66

21) 26
  + 53

22) 63
  + 54

23) 20
  + 98

24) 93
  + 71

25) 74
  + 69

26) 14
  + 87

27) 38
  + 38

28) 60
  + 87

29) 68
  + 80

30) 43
  + 38

Score:

Add these 3 digit numbers.

1)	211 + 224	2)	254 + 150	3)	242 + 227	4)	127 + 202	5)	213 + 198

6)   277   7)   225   8)   148   9)   111   10)   286
     + 190   + 228   + 127   + 120   + 186

11)   255   12)   128   13)   282   14)   310   15)   229
     + 234   + 287   + 172   + 111   + 140

16)   114   17)   333   18)   229   19)   290   20)   163
     + 156   + 123   + 196   + 103   + 288

21)   192   22)   121   23)   126   24)   351   25)   330
     + 135   + 197   + 354   + 107   + 161

26)   110   27)   144   28)   165   29)   151   30)   112
     + 116   + 289   + 283   + 349   + 103

Score:

Addition 0-1000

Add these 3 digit numbers.

1) 250
  + 561

2) 363
  + 209

3) 445
  + 308

4) 301
  + 650

5) 149
  + 817

6) 559
  + 253

7) 336
  + 581

8) 582
  + 156

9) 297
  + 621

10) 465
  + 498

11) 597
  + 254

12) 771
  + 113

13) 551
  + 444

14) 619
  + 115

15) 453
  + 528

16) 574
  + 282

17) 278
  + 297

18) 669
  + 224

19) 492
  + 220

20) 358
  + 189

21) 724
  + 159

22) 357
  + 369

23) 782
  + 151

24) 456
  + 257

25) 265
  + 599

26) 332
  + 280

27) 356
  + 236

28) 499
  + 123

29) 113
  + 130

30) 647
  + 139

Score:

Add these 4 digit numbers.

1)   4,467
+ 3,210
687

2)   1,494
+ 3,034

3)   4,438
+ 1,641

4)   3,049
+ 1,457

5)   4,228
+ 1,344

6)   3,934
+ 1,756

7)   2,360
+ 3,235

8)   2,551
+ 2,719

9)   2,238
+ 227

10)   2,681
+ 1,021

11)   3,362
+ 543

12)   2,053
+ 4,847

13)   4,703
+ 4,077

14)   3,688
+ 4,026

15)   2,592
+ 4,780

16)   1,138
+ 3,408

17)   2,701
+ 3,176

18)   1,300
+ 4,855

19)   4,831
+ 3,005

20)   1,756
+ 3,018

Score:

Adding 3 Numbers

Add these sets of three numbers together in your head.

1)
```
   27
   49
+  24
```

2)
```
   40
   36
+  17
```

3)
```
   21
   47
+  49
```

4)
```
   40
   39
+  14
```

5)
```
   15
   24
+  10
```

6)
```
   39
   13
+  36
```

7)
```
   33
   32
+  41
```

8)
```
   34
   29
+  12
```

9)
```
   16
   15
+   5
```

10)
```
   29
    2
+  28
```

11)
```
   30
   36
+  33
```

12)
```
   46
   20
+  14
```

13)
```
    9
   41
+  23
```

14)
```
   21
   16
+  23
```

15)
```
   39
   46
+  28
```

16)
```
    9
    7
+  12
```

17)
```
   25
   34
+  15
```

18)
```
   25
   31
+  41
```

19)
```
   29
   42
+  21
```

20)
```
   13
   26
+  22
```

18

Score:

Solve these across-down subtraction problems.

1)

79	–	10	–	46	=	
–		–		–		–
22	–	3	–	16	=	
–		–		–		–
20	–	6	–	13	=	
=		=		=		=
	–		–		=	

2)

94	–	34	–	25	=	
–		–		–		–
20	–	6	–	12	=	
–		–		–		–
48	–	20	–	10	=	
=		=		=		=
	–		–		=	

Shade the correct sum.

1)

a) 222   b) 232   c) 221   d) 242   e) 210

–   –   –   –   –

101   102   102   111   102

=   =   =   =   =

112   121   109   231   119

(2)

(1)

Score:

Subtraction 0-100

Subtract these 2 digit numbers.

90s

1)
```
   72
 − 49
 ─────
```

2)
```
   54
 − 22
 ─────
```

3)
```
   92
 − 22
 ─────
```

4)
```
   11
 −  5
 ─────
```

5)
```
   52
 − 40
 ─────
```

6)
```
   23
 − 16
 ─────
```

7)
```
   42
 − 33
 ─────
```

8)
```
   28
 −  8
 ─────
```

9)
```
   80
 − 33
 ─────
```

10)
```
   55
 −  5
 ─────
```

11)
```
   70
 − 62
 ─────
```

12)
```
   67
 − 53
 ─────
```

13)
```
   72
 − 64
 ─────
```

14)
```
   58
 − 51
 ─────
```

15)
```
   55
 − 17
 ─────
```

16)
```
   22
 −  6
 ─────
```

17)
```
   88
 − 28
 ─────
```

18)
```
   27
 − 17
 ─────
```

19)
```
   97
 − 22
 ─────
```

20)
```
   43
 − 36
 ─────
```

21)
```
   38
 − 17
 ─────
```

22)
```
   24
 − 11
 ─────
```

23)
```
   60
 − 31
 ─────
```

24)
```
   92
 − 56
 ─────
```

25)
```
   98
 − 91
 ─────
```

26)
```
   50
 − 22
 ─────
```

27)
```
   62
 − 39
 ─────
```

28)
```
   11
 −  7
 ─────
```

29)
```
   79
 − 30
 ─────
```

30)
```
   38
 −  2
 ─────
```

Time: :

Score:

Subtract the following.

1) 164
  − 12

2) 165
  − 123

3) 136
  − 133

4) 191
  − 38

5) 125
  − 49

6) 125
  − 122

7) 155
  − 126

8) 106
  − 103

9) 177
  − 71

10) 140
  − 116

11) 179
  − 43

12) 191
  − 166

13) 103
  − 45

14) 178
  − 119

15) 162
  − 160

16) 200
  − 124

17) 113
  − 101

18) 132
  − 114

19) 159
  − 147

20) 158
  − 124

21) 123
  − 109

22) 191
  − 94

23) 107
  − 30

24) 114
  − 109

25) 108
  − 95

26) 120
  − 32

27) 181
  − 125

28) 145
  − 20

29) 133
  − 62

30) 192
  − 97

Score:

Subtraction 0-500

Subtract these 3 digit numbers.

1) 205
  − 136

2) 441
  − 253

3) 386
  − 229

4) 455
  − 113

5) 300
  − 180

6) 347
  − 296

7) 205
  − 113

8) 438
  − 257

9) 400
  − 214

10) 271
  − 167

11) 338
  − 288

12) 411
  − 105

13) 397
  − 154

14) 495
  − 307

15) 460
  − 118

16) 355
  − 202

17) 500
  − 215

18) 299
  − 125

19) 230
  − 133

20) 400
  − 119

21) 266
  − 151

22) 378
  − 220

23) 377
  − 291

24) 364
  − 215

25) 422
  − 338

26) 430
  − 215

27) 241
  − 170

28) 258
  − 126

29) 354
  − 247

30) 466
  − 330

Score:

Subtract these 3 digit numbers.

1)
$$\begin{array}{r} 797 \\ -\ 566 \\ \hline \end{array}$$

2)
$$\begin{array}{r} 291 \\ -\ 121 \\ \hline \end{array}$$

3)
$$\begin{array}{r} 882 \\ -\ 713 \\ \hline \end{array}$$

4)
$$\begin{array}{r} 570 \\ -\ 237 \\ \hline \end{array}$$

5)
$$\begin{array}{r} 385 \\ -\ 297 \\ \hline \end{array}$$

6)
$$\begin{array}{r} 323 \\ -\ 118 \\ \hline \end{array}$$

7)
$$\begin{array}{r} 209 \\ -\ 123 \\ \hline \end{array}$$

8)
$$\begin{array}{r} 478 \\ -\ 141 \\ \hline \end{array}$$

9)
$$\begin{array}{r} 489 \\ -\ 222 \\ \hline \end{array}$$

10)
$$\begin{array}{r} 948 \\ -\ 808 \\ \hline \end{array}$$

11)
$$\begin{array}{r} 481 \\ -\ 191 \\ \hline \end{array}$$

12)
$$\begin{array}{r} 268 \\ -\ 103 \\ \hline \end{array}$$

13)
$$\begin{array}{r} 792 \\ -\ 669 \\ \hline \end{array}$$

14)
$$\begin{array}{r} 695 \\ -\ 586 \\ \hline \end{array}$$

15)
$$\begin{array}{r} 431 \\ -\ 234 \\ \hline \end{array}$$

16)
$$\begin{array}{r} 804 \\ -\ 356 \\ \hline \end{array}$$

17)
$$\begin{array}{r} 381 \\ -\ 242 \\ \hline \end{array}$$

18)
$$\begin{array}{r} 512 \\ -\ 334 \\ \hline \end{array}$$

19)
$$\begin{array}{r} 206 \\ -\ 111 \\ \hline \end{array}$$

20)
$$\begin{array}{r} 216 \\ -\ 127 \\ \hline \end{array}$$

21)
$$\begin{array}{r} 428 \\ -\ 284 \\ \hline \end{array}$$

22)
$$\begin{array}{r} 903 \\ -\ 607 \\ \hline \end{array}$$

23)
$$\begin{array}{r} 543 \\ -\ 390 \\ \hline \end{array}$$

24)
$$\begin{array}{r} 342 \\ -\ 102 \\ \hline \end{array}$$

25)
$$\begin{array}{r} 962 \\ -\ 836 \\ \hline \end{array}$$

26)
$$\begin{array}{r} 754 \\ -\ 307 \\ \hline \end{array}$$

27)
$$\begin{array}{r} 494 \\ -\ 363 \\ \hline \end{array}$$

28)
$$\begin{array}{r} 503 \\ -\ 221 \\ \hline \end{array}$$

29)
$$\begin{array}{r} 635 \\ -\ 199 \\ \hline \end{array}$$

30)
$$\begin{array}{r} 466 \\ -\ 376 \\ \hline \end{array}$$

Score:

Subtract these 4 digit numbers.

1) 9,771
  − 8,747

2) 7,598
  − 7,319

3) 1,112
  − 276

4) 3,664
  − 3,435

5) 6,507
  − 1,194

6) 6,013
  − 3,859

7) 7,745
  − 3,156

8) 977
  − 212

9) 5,889
  − 4,757

10) 7,322
  − 4,029

11) 9,438
  − 6,848

12) 346
  − 179

13) 6,619
  − 4,337

14) 8,437
  − 5,165

15) 4,114
  − 1,357

16) 2,447
  − 345

17) 2,433
  − 2,075

18) 7,178
  − 2,337

19) 7,165
  − 1,904

20) 231
  − 131

21) 584
  − 398

22) 5,026
  − 2,448

23) 2,324
  − 1,611

24) 428
  − 173

25) 1,857
  − 1,314

Score:

Calculate the following in your head.

90s

1) 89 + 73 = _____

2) 52 − 49 = _____

3) 64 − 52 = _____

4) 29 + 22 = _____

5) 72 + 31 = _____

6) 62 − 42 = _____

7) 18 + 91 = _____

8) 84 − 44 = _____

9) 99 + 31 = _____

10) 89 + 26 = _____

11) 33 + 57 = _____

12) 98 − 82 = _____

13) 64 − 58 = _____

14) 90 − 87 = _____

15) 99 + 26 = _____

16) 85 − 47 = _____

17) 14 + 68 = _____

18) 58 − 32 = _____

19) 81 − 26 = _____

20) 1 + 40 = _____

21) 79 − 55 = _____

22) 76 − 35 = _____

23) 67 − 2 = _____

24) 72 − 1 = _____

25) 61 + 87 = _____

26) 29 + 28 = _____

27) 81 − 43 = _____

28) 57 + 20 = _____

29) 43 + 53 = _____

30) 45 + 50 = _____

Time: :

25

Score:

Add in plus and minus signs to make the solutions true.

1) $11 + 14\_\_\_\_22\_\_\_\_41 = 88$

2) $18\_\_\_3\_\_\_28 = 49$

3) $2\_\_\_5\_\_\_5 = 2$

4) $2\_\_\_25\_\_\_48 + 14 = 89$

5) $27\_\_\_39 + 8\_\_\_48 = 122$

6) $47\_\_\_1\_\_\_11 = 59$

7) $7\_\_\_37\_\_\_21 = 23$

8) $20\_\_\_35\_\_\_42 = 97$

9) $26\_\_\_39\_\_\_17 = 48$

10) $24\_\_\_22\_\_\_4 = 6$

11) $5\_\_\_1 + 10\_\_\_31 = 47$

12) $16\_\_\_27\_\_\_2 = -13$

13) $14\_\_\_25\_\_\_16 = -27$

14) $12\_\_\_9\_\_\_19 + 49 = 89$

15) $33\_\_\_16\_\_\_18 = 31$

16) $7\_\_\_10\_\_\_13 + 25 = 55$

17) $16\_\_\_4\_\_\_27 = -15$

18) $1\_\_\_21\_\_\_34 = 14$

19) $11\_\_\_3\_\_\_14 = 0$

20) $39\_\_\_31\_\_\_31 = 39$

Score:

Complete these money questions.

1)
$$
\begin{array}{r}
£79.08 \\
-\quad 62.60 \\
\hline
£6.48
\end{array}
$$

2)
$$
\begin{array}{r}
£82.80 \\
-\quad 70.71 \\
\hline
\end{array}
$$

3)
$$
\begin{array}{r}
£58.52 \\
+\quad 90.58 \\
\hline
\end{array}
$$

4)
$$
\begin{array}{r}
£78.35 \\
-\quad 34.97 \\
\hline
\end{array}
$$

5)
$$
\begin{array}{r}
£91.76 \\
-\quad 35.63 \\
\hline
\end{array}
$$

6)
$$
\begin{array}{r}
£82.36 \\
+\quad 98.25 \\
\hline
\end{array}
$$

7)
$$
\begin{array}{r}
£98.63 \\
-\quad 20.98 \\
\hline
\end{array}
$$

8)
$$
\begin{array}{r}
£21.59 \\
+\quad 65.09 \\
\hline
\end{array}
$$

9)
$$
\begin{array}{r}
£70.78 \\
+\quad 41.19 \\
\hline
\end{array}
$$

10)
$$
\begin{array}{r}
£56.10 \\
+\quad 14.79 \\
\hline
\end{array}
$$

11)
$$
\begin{array}{r}
£72.26 \\
-\quad 54.91 \\
\hline
\end{array}
$$

12)
$$
\begin{array}{r}
£86.15 \\
+\quad 99.43 \\
\hline
\end{array}
$$

13)
$$
\begin{array}{r}
£57.35 \\
+\quad 28.92 \\
\hline
\end{array}
$$

14)
$$
\begin{array}{r}
£48.62 \\
+\quad 95.47 \\
\hline
\end{array}
$$

15)
$$
\begin{array}{r}
£93.76 \\
-\quad 29.59 \\
\hline
\end{array}
$$

Complete these money word questions.

1) Richard has £125.50 and buys a new jacket for £101.40. How much money does he have left?

2) Enid is selling theatre tickets for £42 each. She sells six tickets. How much money does Enid make in total?

3) A shirt in a shop costs £35. How much would seven shirts cost?

27

Score:

Counting Tables

Count by -75 from 25 to -3650

1)

25							-500	-575	
	-800		-950	-1,025					
								-2,075	
-2,225							-2,750	-2,825	
									-3,650

Count by 55 from 33 to 2728

2)

33									
						913	968		1,078
	1,188		1,298				1,518		1,628
		1,793							
	2,288								2,728

Score:

Solve these multiplication problems in your head.   60s

1) 3 × 4 = __12__

2) 10 × 4 = __40__

3) 7 × 4 = _____

4) 11 × 4 = __44__

5) 12 × 4 = __48__

6) 9 × 2 = _____

7) 10 × 9 = __90__

8) 10 × 8 = __480__

9) 12 × 9 = _____

10) 4 × 2 = __8__

11) 11 × 2 = __22__

12) 4 × 10 = _____

13) 10 × 12 = __120__

14) 7 × 12 = __84__

15) 8 × 4 = _____

16) 10 × 5 = __50__

17) 3 × 7 = __21__

18) 6 × 0 = _____

19) 6 × 1 = __6__

20) 4 × 6 = __24__

21) 3 × 1 = _____

22) 3 × 6 = __18__

23) 10 × 3 = __30__

24) 11 × 11 = _____

25) 2 × 4 = __8__

26) 1 × 6 = __6__

27) 6 × 2 = _____

28) 11 × 10 = __110__

29) 7 × 5 = _____

30) 7 × 9 = _____

Time: :

Score:

Solve these multiplication word problems.

1) If there are two apples in each box and there are five boxes, how many apples are there in total?

2) Brian swims nine laps every day. How many laps will Brian swim in six days?

3) James has six times more pears than Jake. Jake has four pears. How many pears does James have?

4) Jackie's garden has five rows of pumpkins. Each row has nine pumpkins. How many pumpkins does Jackie have in all?

5) Billy can cycle four miles per hour. How far can Billy cycle in two hours?

Score:

Factors are numbers that be multiplied by another to make a whole number.
List the factors for the numbers below, the first is done for you.

1) 9 _____ 1, 3, 9 _____   2) 5 _____

3) 8 _____   4) 21 _____

5) 35 _____   6) 1 _____

7) 6 _____   8) 17 _____

9) 7 _____   10) 99 _____

(9)

Common Factors are numbers that are factors of two numbers.
List the factors for the numbers below, adding common factors in the
centre of the Venn diagram.

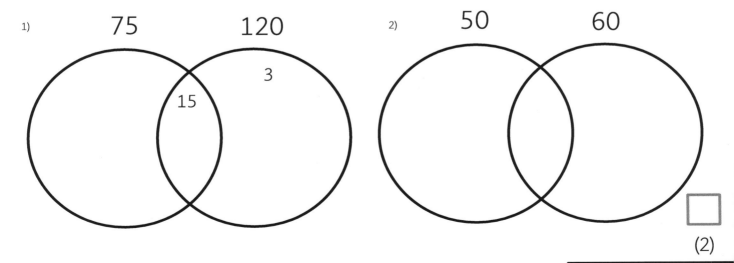

1) 75   120

15   3

2) 50   60

(2)

Score:

Multiples

A multiple is a number that can be divided by another number with no remainder. List the first five for each of the questions below, one is done for you.

1) 10   10, 20, 30, 40, 50

2) 13 _____

3) 14 _____

4) 4 _____

5) 7 _____

6) 1 _____

7) 8 _____

8) 2 _____

9) 5 _____

10) 12 _____

☐ (9)

Common multiples are numbers that can be divided by two numbers (again with no remainder). Write down the first six multiples for these numbers, adding common multiples in the centre of the Venn diagram.

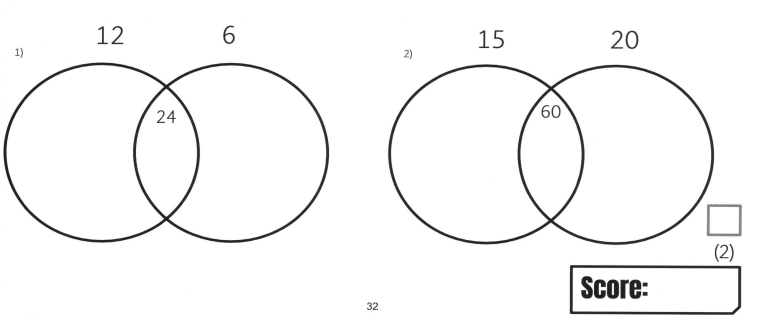

1)   12   6

24

2)   15   20

60

☐ (2)

Score:

32

List the factors for each number. Is the number prime?

1) 60 = <u>2,3,5 (Not prime)</u>   2) 43 = _____   3) 94 = _____

4) 76 = _____   5) 85 = _____   6) 31 = _____

7) 68 = _____   8) 13 = _____   9) 18 = _____

10) 61 = _____   11) 90 = _____   12) 41 = _____

Read these sentences and then add the prime number it describes between 0 and 100. It will help to have the possible answers written out in front of you.

(11)

1) It is less than 50 and its digits add up to 8.

2) It is a two digit number and is a factor of 99.

3) A harder one: Its digits add up to 16 and it is 6 more than the previous prime number.

(3)

Score:

Long Multiplication

Use long multiplication to solve these problems.

1)
```
    62
×    5
_____
```

2)
```
    46
×    7
_____
```

3)
```
    39
×    8
_____
```

4)
```
    70
×    7
_____
```

5)
```
    88
×   11
_____
```

6)
```
    55
×    6
_____
```

7)
```
    23
×   35
_____
```

8)
```
    32
×    4
_____
```

9)
```
    27
×    7
_____
```

10)
```
    83
×   75
_____
```

11)
```
    67
×    5
_____
```

12)
```
    35
×    7
_____
```

13)
```
    28
×   58
_____
```

14)
```
    98
×   22
_____
```

15)
```
    57
×   36
_____
```

16)
```
    30
×   12
_____
```

17)
```
    85
×   42
_____
```

18)
```
    25
×    9
_____
```

19)
```
    57
×   88
_____
```

20)
```
    74
×   44
_____
```

21)
```
    99
×    2
_____
```

22)
```
    57
×    3
_____
```

23)
```
    91
×   14
_____
```

24)
```
    64
×    2
_____
```

25)
```
    38
×    0
_____
```

26)
```
    86
×    6
_____
```

27)
```
    65
×   75
_____
```

28)
```
    85
×   50
_____
```

29)
```
    17
×   82
_____
```

30)
```
    17
×   91
_____
```

34

Score:

Use long multiplication to solve these problems.

1)
```
   836
 ×   6
_____
```

2)
```
   623
 ×  42
_____
```

3)
```
   283
 ×  82
_____
```

4)
```
   901
 ×  63
_____
```

5)
```
    13
 ×  80
_____
```

6)
```
   359
 ×  71
_____
```

7)
```
   301
 ×  22
_____
```

8)
```
   282
 ×  54
_____
```

9)
```
   462
 ×   8
_____
```

10)
```
   906
 ×  92
_____
```

11)
```
    40
 ×  54
_____
```

12)
```
   215
 ×   8
_____
```

13)
```
   704
 ×   9
_____
```

14)
```
   645
 ×   5
_____
```

15)
```
    61
 ×  92
_____
```

16)
```
   600
 ×   5
_____
```

17)
```
   112
 ×   7
_____
```

18)
```
   778
 ×  54
_____
```

19)
```
    65
 ×   6
_____
```

20)
```
   507
 ×  50
_____
```

Score:

Long Multiplication

Use long multiplication to solve these problems.

1) 6,617
 ×   12

2) 1,101
 ×   5

3) 6,659
 ×   73

4) 8,981
 ×   36

5) 7,231
 ×   8

6) 2,898
 ×   74

7) 5,243
 ×   98

8) 5,082
 ×   83

9) 4,131
 ×   9

10) 8,209
 ×   37

11) 9,855
 ×   7

12) 5,741
 ×   43

13) 3,162
 ×   6

14) 5,747
 ×   22

15) 1,443
 ×   57

16) 6,369
 ×   67

17) 4,841
 ×   6

18) 3,711
 ×   4

19) 1,104
 ×   26

20) 2,280
 ×   21

Score:

Solve these division problems in your head.

60s

1) 27 ÷ 3 = _____

2) 8 ÷ 8 = _____

3) 81 ÷ 9 = _____

4) 30 ÷ 5 = _____

5) 66 ÷ 6 = _____

6) 72 ÷ 9 = _____

7) 6 ÷ 2 = _____

8) 88 ÷ 11 = _____

9) 20 ÷ 2 = _____

10) 24 ÷ 8 = _____

11) 56 ÷ 7 = _____

12) 33 ÷ 3 = _____

13) 22 ÷ 11 = _____

14) 20 ÷ 5 = _____

15) 21 ÷ 7 = _____

16) 60 ÷ 6 = _____

17) 18 ÷ 6 = _____

18) 15 ÷ 5 = _____

19) 63 ÷ 9 = _____

20) 40 ÷ 4 = _____

21) 12 ÷ 3 = _____

22) 25 ÷ 5 = _____

23) 44 ÷ 4 = _____

24) 9 ÷ 1 = _____

25) 45 ÷ 9 = _____

26) 42 ÷ 6 = _____

27) 6 ÷ 1 = _____

28) 63 ÷ 7 = _____

29) 60 ÷ 10 = _____

30) 40 ÷ 10 = _____

Time: :

Score:

Solve these division word problems.

1) Paul ordered four pizzas. The bill for the pizzas came to $36. What was the cost of each pizza?

2) Brian is reading a book with 72 pages. If Brian wants to read the same number of pages every day, how many pages would Brian have to read each day to finish in nine days?

3) A box of bananas weighs six pounds. If one banana weighs two pounds, how many bananas are there in the box?

4) How many six cm pieces of rope can you cut from a rope that is 48 cm long?

5) You have 28 peaches and want to share them equally with four people. How many peaches would each person get?

Score:

Solve these remainder problems.

1)

$$6\overline{)136}$$

2)

$$6\overline{)681}$$

3)

$$7\overline{)547}$$

4)

$$9\overline{)759}$$

5)

$$8\overline{)129}$$

6)

$$8\overline{)73}$$

7)

$$2\overline{)122}$$

8)

$$4\overline{)79}$$

9)

$$1\overline{)958}$$

10)

$$8\overline{)840}$$

11)

$$3\overline{)709}$$

12)

$$8\overline{)471}$$

13)

$$2\overline{)957}$$

14)

$$6\overline{)364}$$

15)

$$4\overline{)428}$$

16)

$$4\overline{)329}$$

17)

$$4\overline{)295}$$

18)

$$5\overline{)81}$$

19)

$$5\overline{)237}$$

20)

$$5\overline{)837}$$

21)

$$6\overline{)583}$$

22)

$$9\overline{)380}$$

23)

$$3\overline{)126}$$

24)

$$9\overline{)126}$$

25)

$$6\overline{)254}$$

26)

$$1\overline{)325}$$

27)

$$7\overline{)892}$$

28)

$$8\overline{)519}$$

29)

$$7\overline{)104}$$

30)

$$5\overline{)624}$$

Score:

Remainders 2

Solve these remainder problems.

1) $2\overline{)3{,}907}$

2) $7\overline{)5{,}446}$

3) $7\overline{)6{,}045}$

4) $7\overline{)6{,}072}$

5) $6\overline{)175}$

6) $5\overline{)1{,}139}$

7) $4\overline{)1{,}793}$

8) $2\overline{)2{,}359}$

9) $5\overline{)8{,}312}$

10) $7\overline{)7{,}834}$

11) $4\overline{)9{,}382}$

12) $7\overline{)3{,}792}$

13) $3\overline{)975}$

14) $5\overline{)4{,}415}$

15) $2\overline{)8{,}643}$

16) $5\overline{)3{,}757}$

17) $4\overline{)8{,}432}$

18) $5\overline{)1{,}084}$

19) $6\overline{)442}$

20) $4\overline{)3{,}470}$

21) $4\overline{)6{,}491}$

22) $6\overline{)9{,}411}$

23) $8\overline{)5{,}323}$

24) $5\overline{)8{,}606}$

25) $4\overline{)5{,}275}$

26) $6\overline{)931}$

27) $8\overline{)9{,}887}$

28) $9\overline{)5{,}455}$

29) $7\overline{)7{,}476}$

30) $4\overline{)6{,}085}$

Score:

Complete the diamond problems. The top cell contains the product of the number in the right and left cells and the bottom cell contains the sum. The first one has been done.

1)
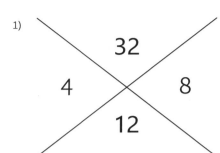

32

4   8

12

2)
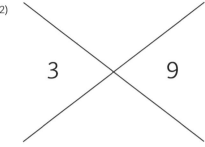

3   9

3)
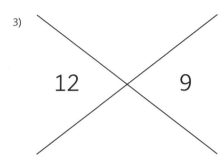

12   9

4)
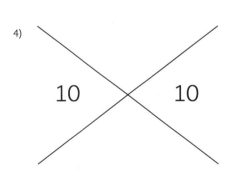

10   10

5)
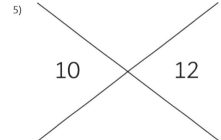

10   12

6)
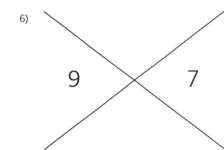

9   7

7)
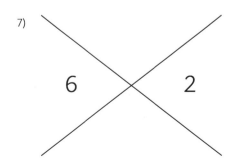

6   2

8)
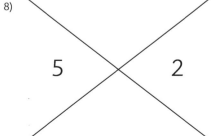

5   2

9)
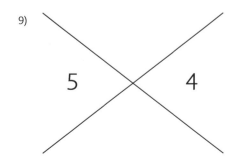

5   4

41

Score:

Multiplication Boxes

Fill in these multiplication boxes. Each row, column and diagonal can be multiplied to make the outer numbers.

1)

			21
		1	7
10			120
	8	8	448
490	24	32	168

2)

			192
9			252
	8		288
6	5		270
216	280	324	648

3)

			180
6		6	36
			90
5		2	90
150	54	36	72

4)

			60
	4		120
	4		48
3		6	54
36	48	180	144

5)

			36
		9	405
8		8	64
		4	32
160	18	288	20

6)

			30
4			36
7			210
	2	8	32
56	30	144	160

42

Score:

Multiply out these powers of ten.

1)
$$\begin{array}{r} 1.5 \\ \times\ 1{,}000 \\ \hline \end{array}$$

2)
$$\begin{array}{r} 99 \\ \times\ 100 \\ \hline \end{array}$$

3)
$$\begin{array}{r} 17 \\ \times\ 1{,}000 \\ \hline \end{array}$$

4)
$$\begin{array}{r} 1.7 \\ \times\ 1{,}000 \\ \hline \end{array}$$

5)
$$\begin{array}{r} 21 \\ \times\ 1{,}000 \\ \hline \end{array}$$

6)
$$\begin{array}{r} 21 \\ \times\ 100 \\ \hline \end{array}$$

7)
$$\begin{array}{r} 7.7 \\ \times\ 10 \\ \hline \end{array}$$

8)
$$\begin{array}{r} 7.7 \\ \times\ 1{,}000 \\ \hline \end{array}$$

9)
$$\begin{array}{r} 4.8 \\ \times\ 10 \\ \hline \end{array}$$

10)
$$\begin{array}{r} 7.7 \\ \times\ 100 \\ \hline \end{array}$$

11)
$$\begin{array}{r} 0.4 \\ \times\ 10 \\ \hline \end{array}$$

12)
$$\begin{array}{r} 6.5 \\ \times\ 1{,}000 \\ \hline \end{array}$$

13)
$$\begin{array}{r} 5.5 \\ \times\ 10 \\ \hline \end{array}$$

14)
$$\begin{array}{r} 6.3 \\ \times\ 10 \\ \hline \end{array}$$

15)
$$\begin{array}{r} 25 \\ \times\ 100 \\ \hline \end{array}$$

16)
$$\begin{array}{r} 8.6 \\ \times\ 100 \\ \hline \end{array}$$

17)
$$\begin{array}{r} 5.7 \\ \times\ 10 \\ \hline \end{array}$$

18)
$$\begin{array}{r} 62 \\ \times\ 10 \\ \hline \end{array}$$

19)
$$\begin{array}{r} 11 \\ \times\ 1{,}000 \\ \hline \end{array}$$

20)
$$\begin{array}{r} 8.8 \\ \times\ 100 \\ \hline \end{array}$$

21)
$$\begin{array}{r} 7.2 \\ \times\ 10 \\ \hline \end{array}$$

22)
$$\begin{array}{r} 64 \\ \times\ 10 \\ \hline \end{array}$$

23)
$$\begin{array}{r} 4.4 \\ \times\ 10 \\ \hline \end{array}$$

24)
$$\begin{array}{r} 0.3 \\ \times\ 100 \\ \hline \end{array}$$

25)
$$\begin{array}{r} 8.9 \\ \times\ 100 \\ \hline \end{array}$$

26)
$$\begin{array}{r} 6 \\ \times\ 10 \\ \hline \end{array}$$

27)
$$\begin{array}{r} 0.6 \\ \times\ 1{,}000 \\ \hline \end{array}$$

28)
$$\begin{array}{r} 7.5 \\ \times\ 10 \\ \hline \end{array}$$

29)
$$\begin{array}{r} 89 \\ \times\ 10 \\ \hline \end{array}$$

30)
$$\begin{array}{r} 5.9 \\ \times\ 100 \\ \hline \end{array}$$

Score:

Divide by 10 or 100.

1)

$$100\overline{)754}$$

2)

$$10\overline{)371}$$

3)

$$10\overline{)214}$$

4)

$$10\overline{)169}$$

5)

$$100\overline{)771}$$

6)

$$100\overline{)187}$$

7)

$$100\overline{)886}$$

8)

$$10\overline{)987}$$

9)

$$10\overline{)306}$$

10)

$$10\overline{)573}$$

11)

$$100\overline{)668}$$

12)

$$100\overline{)690}$$

13)

$$100\overline{)659}$$

14)

$$10\overline{)154}$$

15)

$$10\overline{)186}$$

16)

$$100\overline{)595}$$

17)

$$10\overline{)478}$$

18)

$$100\overline{)424}$$

19)

$$100\overline{)538}$$

20)

$$10\overline{)410}$$

Score:

Square these values.

1) $2^2 =$ _____

2) $11^2 =$ _____

3) $12^2 =$ _____

4) $10^2 =$ _____

5) $9^2 =$ _____

6) $1^2 =$ _____

7) $5^2 =$ _____

8) $6^2 =$ _____

9) $7^2 =$ _____

10) $3^2 =$ _____

11) $4^2 =$ _____

12) $8^2 =$ _____

Cube these values.

1) $12^3 =$ _____

2) $2^3 =$ _____

3) $7^3 =$ _____

4) $11^3 =$ _____

5) $10^3 =$ _____

6) $5^3 =$ _____

7) $4^3 =$ _____

8) $3^3 =$ _____

9) $1^3 =$ _____

10) $8^3 =$ _____

11) $9^3 =$ _____

12) $6^3 =$ _____

Score:

Mixed Operations

Calculate the following in your head.

75s

1) 4 × 6 = __24__

2) 12 × 6 = __72__

3) 8 × 5 = __40__

4) 1 × 11 = __11__

5) 45 − 39 = _____

6) 38 − 14 = _____

7) 79 − 61 = _____

8) 34 − 10 = _____

9) 7 × 3 = _____

10) 1 × 5 = _____

11) 46 − 13 = _____

12) 56 ÷ 7 = _____

13) 44 ÷ 11 = _____

14) 24 − 14 = _____

15) 3 × 5 = _____

16) 12 ÷ 3 = _____

17) 98 + 43 = _____

18) 12 ÷ 2 = _____

19) 52 + 34 = _____

20) 36 + 51 = _____

21) 84 + 77 = _____

22) 60 ÷ 12 = _____

23) 22 ÷ 2 = _____

24) 74 − 33 = _____

25) 55 + 87 = _____

26) 94 + 81 = _____

27) 28 ÷ 7 = _____

28) 73 + 87 = _____

29) 26 + 75 = _____

30) 20 − 11 = _____

Time: ____ : ____

Score: ____

Identify the Fraction as per the shaded rectangles.

1) 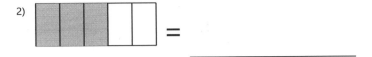 =

_____

2)  =

_____

3)  =

_____

4) 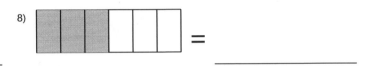 =

_____

5) 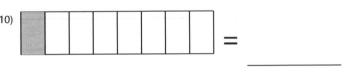 =

_____

6) 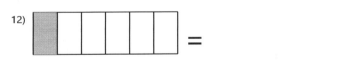 =

_____

7) 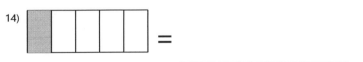 =

_____

8) 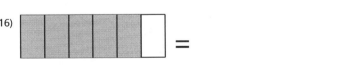 =

_____

9)  =

_____

10) 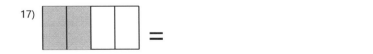 =

_____

11) 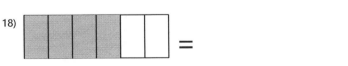 =

_____

12) 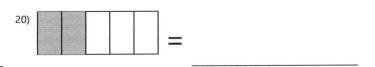 =

_____

13) =

_____

14) =

_____

15) =

_____

16) =

_____

17) =

_____

18) =

_____

19) =

_____

20) =

_____

Fraction Identification

Identify the Fraction as per the shaded blocks.

1) 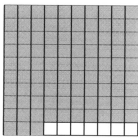 = _____

2) 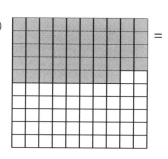 = _____

3) 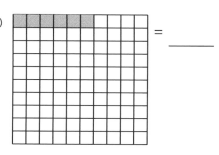 = _____

4) 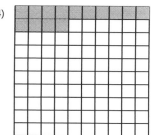 = _____

5) 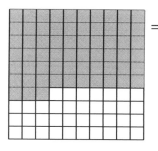 = _____

6) 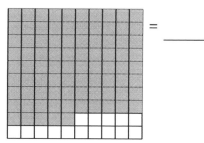 = _____

7) 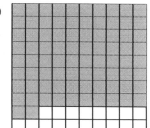 = _____

8) 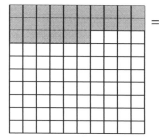 = _____

9) 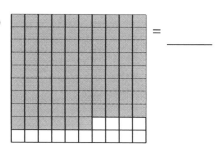 = _____

10) 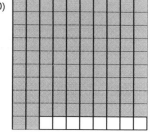 = _____

11) 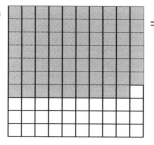 = _____

12) 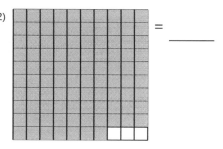 = _____

13) 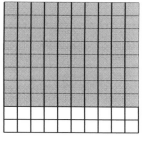 = _____

14) 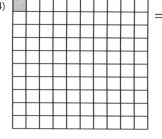 = _____

15) 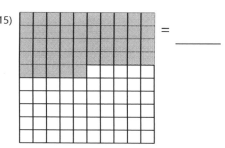 = _____

Score:

48

Simplify these fractions.

1) $\dfrac{8}{40} =$ $\dfrac{4}{20}$

2) $\dfrac{16}{24} =$ _____

3) $\dfrac{30}{40} =$ _____

4) $\dfrac{12}{18} =$ _____

5) $\dfrac{10}{25} =$ _____

6) $\dfrac{21}{28} =$ _____

7) $\dfrac{5}{40} =$ _____

8) $\dfrac{4}{12} =$ _____

9) $\dfrac{6}{15} =$ _____

10) $\dfrac{15}{18} =$ _____

11) $\dfrac{18}{27} =$ _____

12) $\dfrac{6}{24} =$ _____

13) $\dfrac{12}{24} =$ _____

14) $\dfrac{6}{18} =$ _____

15) $\dfrac{8}{12} =$ _____

16) $\dfrac{4}{32} =$ _____

17) $\dfrac{18}{45} =$ _____

18) $\dfrac{3}{9} =$ _____

19) $\dfrac{2}{10} =$ _____

20) $\dfrac{14}{16} =$ _____

21) $\dfrac{9}{12} =$ _____

22) $\dfrac{3}{15} =$ _____

23) $\dfrac{14}{28} =$ _____

24) $\dfrac{10}{16} =$ _____

25) $\dfrac{4}{20} =$ _____

26) $\dfrac{6}{12} =$ _____

27) $\dfrac{7}{21} =$ _____

28) $\dfrac{15}{40} =$ _____

29) $\dfrac{2}{6} =$ _____

30) $\dfrac{25}{30} =$ _____

Score:

Comparing Fractions

Compare the fractions. Add <, > or =.

1) $\dfrac{3}{4} > \dfrac{2}{4}$

2) $\dfrac{1}{3} < \dfrac{2}{3}$

3) $\dfrac{1}{6} < \dfrac{4}{6}$

4) $\dfrac{3}{10} < \dfrac{9}{10}$

5) $\dfrac{3}{4} > \dfrac{1}{4}$

6) $\dfrac{1}{2} = \dfrac{1}{2}$

7) $\dfrac{4}{8} < \dfrac{6}{8}$

8) $\dfrac{2}{5} < \dfrac{3}{5}$

9) $\dfrac{4}{6} < \dfrac{5}{6}$

10) $\dfrac{1}{10} = \dfrac{1}{10}$

11) $\dfrac{4}{5} > \dfrac{1}{5}$

12) $\dfrac{2}{3} = \dfrac{2}{3}$

13) $\dfrac{6}{8} > \dfrac{4}{8}$

14) $\dfrac{2}{4} > \dfrac{1}{4}$

15) $\dfrac{7}{8} > \dfrac{1}{8}$

16) $\dfrac{2}{6} < \dfrac{4}{6}$

17) $\dfrac{5}{10} > \dfrac{3}{10}$

18) $\dfrac{3}{5} > \dfrac{1}{5}$

19) $\dfrac{3}{5} = \dfrac{3}{5}$

20) $\dfrac{2}{3} > \dfrac{1}{3}$

Now try for different denominators.

1) $\dfrac{1}{8} \underline{\quad} \dfrac{2}{3}$

2) $\dfrac{1}{4} \underline{\quad} \dfrac{3}{5}$

3) $\dfrac{1}{2} \underline{\quad} \dfrac{2}{10}$

4) $\dfrac{4}{6} \underline{\quad} \dfrac{1}{4}$

5) $\dfrac{1}{2} \underline{\quad} \dfrac{2}{3}$

6) $\dfrac{2}{6} \underline{\quad} \dfrac{3}{10}$

7) $\dfrac{3}{8} \underline{\quad} \dfrac{1}{5}$

8) $\dfrac{1}{5} \underline{\quad} \dfrac{1}{3}$

9) $\dfrac{1}{2} \underline{\quad} \dfrac{8}{10}$

10) $\dfrac{4}{6} \underline{\quad} \dfrac{2}{4}$

11) $\dfrac{1}{8} \underline{\quad} \dfrac{4}{5}$

12) $\dfrac{5}{10} \underline{\quad} \dfrac{2}{8}$

13) $\dfrac{1}{3} \underline{\quad} \dfrac{1}{2}$

14) $\dfrac{3}{6} \underline{\quad} \dfrac{2}{4}$

15) $\dfrac{1}{2} \underline{\quad} \dfrac{3}{8}$

16) $\dfrac{3}{10} \underline{\quad} \dfrac{2}{6}$

17) $\dfrac{2}{3} \underline{\quad} \dfrac{1}{5}$

18) $\dfrac{1}{4} \underline{\quad} \dfrac{2}{6}$

19) $\dfrac{2}{8} \underline{\quad} \dfrac{5}{10}$

20) $\dfrac{2}{4} \underline{\quad} \dfrac{1}{2}$

Score:

50

Add these fractions together, writing your answer in the lowest terms.

1) $\dfrac{2}{4}$
   $+ \dfrac{1}{2}$

2) $\dfrac{7}{8}$
   $+ \dfrac{3}{4}$

3) $\dfrac{3}{10}$
   $+ \dfrac{3}{10}$

4) $\dfrac{1}{6}$
   $+ \dfrac{1}{2}$

5) $\dfrac{1}{2}$
   $+ \dfrac{1}{6}$

6) $\dfrac{3}{10}$
   $+ \dfrac{3}{4}$

7) $\dfrac{5}{10}$
   $+ \dfrac{1}{10}$

8) $\dfrac{2}{4}$
   $+ \dfrac{3}{8}$

9) $\dfrac{1}{2}$
   $+ \dfrac{4}{6}$

10) $\dfrac{3}{8}$
    $+ \dfrac{5}{8}$

11) $\dfrac{3}{4}$
    $+ \dfrac{9}{12}$

12) $\dfrac{5}{8}$
    $+ \dfrac{1}{2}$

13) $\dfrac{3}{8}$
    $+ \dfrac{3}{4}$

14) $\dfrac{1}{3}$
    $+ \dfrac{5}{6}$

15) $\dfrac{2}{4}$
    $+ \dfrac{1}{2}$

16) $\dfrac{3}{5}$
    $+ \dfrac{3}{10}$

17) $\dfrac{6}{8}$
    $+ \dfrac{3}{4}$

18) $\dfrac{3}{4}$
    $+ \dfrac{5}{8}$

19) $\dfrac{7}{12}$
    $+ \dfrac{3}{4}$

20) $\dfrac{7}{8}$
    $+ \dfrac{1}{2}$

Score:

Subtracting Fractions

Subtract these fractions, writing your answer in the lowest terms.

1) $\frac{6}{10} - \frac{2}{5}$

2) $\frac{12}{20} - \frac{5}{20}$

3) $\frac{3}{5} - \frac{4}{10}$

4) $\frac{12}{20} - \frac{2}{4}$

5) $\frac{1}{2} - \frac{1}{4}$

6) $\frac{6}{12} - \frac{2}{6}$

7) $\frac{10}{12} - \frac{1}{3}$

8) $\frac{9}{10} - \frac{1}{2}$

9) $\frac{1}{2} - \frac{2}{20}$

10) $\frac{14}{15} - \frac{2}{5}$

11) $\frac{2}{3} - \frac{3}{6}$

12) $\frac{3}{4} - \frac{1}{2}$

13) $\frac{7}{15} - \frac{6}{15}$

14) $\frac{8}{10} - \frac{6}{10}$

15) $\frac{2}{3} - \frac{1}{3}$

16) $\frac{7}{8} - \frac{3}{4}$

17) $\frac{9}{10} - \frac{4}{5}$

18) $\frac{9}{15} - \frac{1}{15}$

19) $\frac{3}{20} - \frac{1}{10}$

20) $\frac{2}{3} - \frac{3}{15}$

Score:

Convert these mixed numbers to improper fractions, and vice versa.

1) $\dfrac{30}{4}$ = _____

2) $\dfrac{33}{8}$ = _____

3) $6\dfrac{1}{5}$ = _____

4) $6\dfrac{4}{6}$ = _____

5) $1\dfrac{2}{8}$ = _____

6) $\dfrac{25}{6}$ = _____

7) $1\dfrac{2}{4}$ = _____

8) $8\dfrac{4}{5}$ = _____

9) $7\dfrac{1}{6}$ = _____

10) $1\dfrac{3}{5}$ = _____

11) $4\dfrac{5}{6}$ = _____

12) $\dfrac{19}{3}$ = _____

13) $5\dfrac{4}{5}$ = _____

14) $\dfrac{38}{8}$ = _____

15) $\dfrac{23}{3}$ = _____

16) $9\dfrac{1}{8}$ = _____

17) $2\dfrac{1}{6}$ = _____

18) $\dfrac{19}{4}$ = _____

19) $9\dfrac{4}{5}$ = _____

20) $\dfrac{21}{4}$ = _____

21) $9\dfrac{1}{4}$ = _____

22) $\dfrac{34}{8}$ = _____

23) $\dfrac{51}{6}$ = _____

24) $\dfrac{9}{6}$ = _____

25) $8\dfrac{5}{8}$ = _____

26) $6\dfrac{4}{5}$ = _____

27) $5\dfrac{3}{4}$ = _____

28) $6\dfrac{2}{3}$ = _____

29) $\dfrac{62}{8}$ = _____

30) $1\dfrac{1}{3}$ = _____

Score:

53

Multiplying Fractions

Multiply these fractions and whole numbers.

1) $\frac{1}{5}$ of 5 = _____

2) $6 \times \frac{4}{6}$ = _____

3) $8 \times \frac{5}{8}$ = _____

4) $\frac{1}{4}$ of 4 = _____

5) $6 \times \frac{2}{6}$ = _____

6) $3 \times \frac{2}{3}$ = _____

7) $\frac{6}{8}$ of 8 = _____

8) $\frac{3}{5}$ of 5 = _____

9) $6 \times \frac{2}{3}$ = _____

10) $\frac{2}{8}$ of 8 = _____

11) $6 \times \frac{2}{6}$ = _____

12) $5 \times \frac{2}{5}$ = _____

13) $6 \times \frac{3}{6}$ = _____

14) $\frac{2}{3}$ of 6 = _____

15) $\frac{7}{8}$ of 8 = _____

16) $\frac{2}{4}$ of 4 = _____

17) $\frac{4}{8}$ of 8 = _____

18) $\frac{3}{4}$ of 4 = _____

19) $3 \times \frac{1}{3}$ = _____

20) $6 \times \frac{4}{6}$ = _____

21) $6 \times \frac{1}{6}$ = _____

22) $3 \times \frac{1}{3}$ = _____

23) $\frac{3}{8}$ of 8 = _____

24) $5 \times \frac{4}{5}$ = _____

25) $8 \times \frac{5}{8}$ = _____

26) $6 \times \frac{3}{6}$ = _____

27) $\frac{2}{5}$ of 5 = _____

28) $3 \times \frac{1}{3}$ = _____

29) $3 \times \frac{2}{3}$ = _____

30) $6 \times \frac{2}{6}$ = _____

Score:

Convert these fractions to decimals.

1) $\dfrac{6}{10} = $ _____

2) $\dfrac{90}{100} = $ _____

3) $\dfrac{3}{25} = $ _____

4) $\dfrac{13}{20} = $ _____

5) $\dfrac{2}{4} = $ _____

6) $\dfrac{36}{50} = $ _____

7) $\dfrac{1}{5} = $ _____

8) $\dfrac{15}{100} = $ _____

9) $\dfrac{1}{2} = $ _____

10) $\dfrac{2}{20} = $ _____

11) $\dfrac{35}{50} = $ _____

12) $\dfrac{4}{5} = $ _____

13) $\dfrac{5}{10} = $ _____

14) $\dfrac{17}{25} = $ _____

15) $\dfrac{14}{25} = $ _____

16) $\dfrac{48}{100} = $ _____

17) $\dfrac{3}{10} = $ _____

18) $\dfrac{10}{20} = $ _____

19) $\dfrac{31}{50} = $ _____

20) $\dfrac{3}{5} = $ _____

21) $\dfrac{1}{4} = $ _____

22) $\dfrac{9}{10} = $ _____

23) $\dfrac{8}{20} = $ _____

24) $\dfrac{49}{50} = $ _____

25) $\dfrac{33}{100} = $ _____

26) $\dfrac{2}{5} = $ _____

27) $\dfrac{15}{20} = $ _____

28) $\dfrac{12}{25} = $ _____

29) $\dfrac{96}{100} = $ _____

30) $\dfrac{24}{50} = $ _____

55

Score:

Decimals to Fractions

Convert these decimals to fractions (and simplify).

1) $0.85 = $ _____

2) $0.5 = $ _____

3) $0.55 = $ _____

4) $0.2 = $ _____

5) $0.08 = $ _____

6) $0.26 = $ _____

7) $0.6 = $ _____

8) $0.25 = $ _____

9) $0.8 = $ _____

10) $0.66 = $ _____

11) $0.24 = $ _____

12) $0.32 = $ _____

13) $0.52 = $ _____

14) $0.4 = $ _____

15) $0.36 = $ _____

16) $0.76 = $ _____

17) $0.3 = $ _____

18) $0.88 = $ _____

19) $0.9 = $ _____

20) $0.46 = $ _____

21) $0.37 = $ _____

22) $0.15 = $ _____

23) $0.17 = $ _____

24) $0.1 = $ _____

25) $0.7 = $ _____

26) $0.12 = $ _____

27) $0.95 = $ _____

28) $0.48 = $ _____

29) $0.68 = $ _____

30) $0.86 = $ _____

Score: _____

Round to the underlined digit. The first one is done for you.

1) £6<u>9</u>.26 = <u>£69.00</u>

2) £378.<u>8</u>4 = _____

3) £72<u>0</u>.88 = _____

4) £47<u>8</u>.34 = _____

5) £<u>5</u>79.27 = _____

6) £<u>7</u>72.42 = _____

7) £9<u>7</u>3.01 = _____

8) £3<u>1</u>.46 = _____

9) £<u>7</u>2.93 = _____

10) £1<u>6</u>9.52 = _____

11) £2<u>0</u>4.07 = _____

12) £89<u>3</u>.15 = _____

13) £496.<u>6</u>6 = _____

14) £529.<u>2</u>7 = _____

15) £96<u>9</u>.89 = _____

16) £8<u>3</u>7.77 = _____

17) £90<u>1</u>.60 = _____

18) £722.<u>2</u>4 = _____

19) £350.<u>0</u>9 = _____

20) £9<u>3</u>9.15 = _____

Score:

Convert these decimals to percentages and vice versa.

1) 0.35 = __35%__

2) 0.59 = _____

3) 46 % = _____

4) 32 % = __0.32__

5) 80 % = _____

6) 0.53 = _____

7) 43 % = __0.43__

8) 0.62 = _____

9) 0.64 = _____

10) 98 % = __0.98__

11) 0.67 = _____

12) 0.02 = _____

13) 63 % = __0.63__

14) 0.17 = _____

15) 0.69 = _____

16) 0.22 = __22,__

17) 0.7 = _____

18) 0.68 = _____

19) 94 % = __0.94__

20) 55 % = _____

21) 25 % = _____

22) 0.21 = __21__

23) 0.74 = _____

24) 65 % = _____

25) 9 % = __0-09__

26) 75 % = _____

27) 71 % = _____

28) 57 % = _____

29) 11 % = _____

30) 0.39 = _____

Score:

Convert these measurements.

1) 83 ml = _____ l

2) 66 l = _____ ml

3) 54 l = _____ ml

4) 33 l = _____ ml

5) 75 l = _____ ml

6) 27 ml = _____ l

7) 88 l = _____ ml

8) 79 l = _____ ml

9) 25 l = _____ ml

10) 22 l = _____ ml

11) 23 ml = _____ l

12) 21 ml = _____ l

13) 58 l = _____ ml

14) 22 ml = _____ l

15) 84 ml = _____ l

16) 63 l = _____ ml

17) 72 ml = _____ l

18) 73 ml = _____ l

19) 95 ml = _____ l

20) 71 ml = _____ l

Score:

Convert these measurements.

1) 27 ml = _____ l   2) 46 ml = _____ l

3) 70 l = _____ ml   4) 24 ml = _____ l

5) 92 l = _____ ml   6) 33 ml = _____ l

7) 20 ml = _____ l   8) 91 l = _____ ml

9) 82 l = _____ ml   10) 96 l = _____ ml

William has a 900 ml jug of orange squash; 850ml of water and 50ml of concentrate.

1) As a simplified fraction, what portion of the orange squash is water?

2) A pint is 473.176 ml. To the nearest whole number, how many pints of squash are there?

3) William drinks 311ml of squash. How much squash is left in the jug (in ml)?

Score:

Shade in the temperature for each thermometer (in celsius).

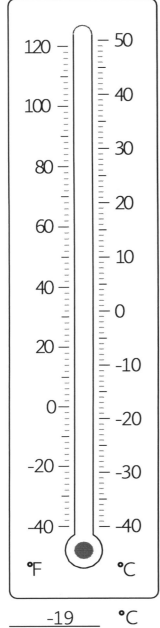

1)

°F	°C

_____-19_____ °C

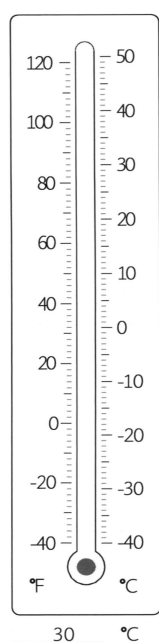

2)

°F	°C

_____30_____ °C

3)

°F	°C

_____46_____ °C

4) What is the difference in Celsius between the hottest and coolest thermometer?

_____

Score:

Identify the temperature for each thermometer (in celsius).

1)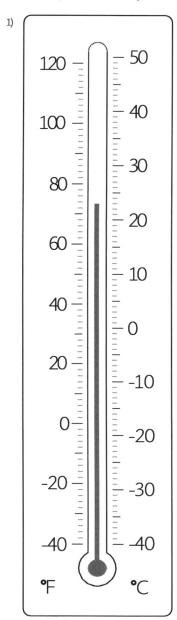

2)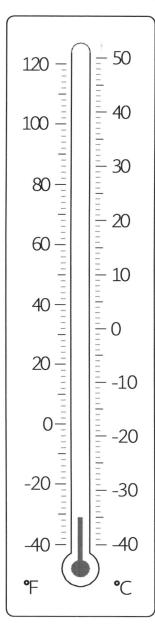

3)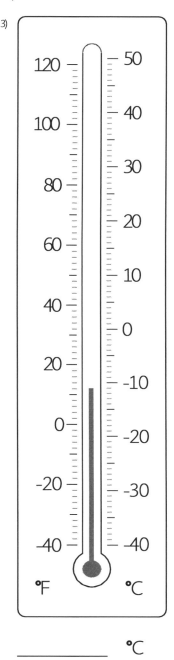

_____ °C   _____ °C   _____ °C

4) Which thermometer was hottest?

Score:

Draw the clock hands to show the passage of time.

1)

What time will it be in 3 hours 33 minutes?

2)

What time was it 5 hours 53 minutes ago?

3)

What time was it 5 hours 21 minutes ago?

4)

What time was it 5 hours 50 minutes ago?

5)

What time will it be in 3 hours 16 minutes?

6)

What time will it be in 1 hour 50 minutes?

7)

What time was it 3 hours 31 minutes ago?

8)

What time will it be in 3 hours 24 minutes?

Score:

Convert the given measures of time to alternate measures of time.

1) 76 hours = _____ days _____ hours

2) 80 min = _____ secs

3) 15 days = _____ hours

4) 77 days = _____ weeks

5) 80 secs = _____ min _____ secs

6) 40 hours = _____ mins

7) 21 hours = _____ mins

8) 12 mins = _____ secs

9) 88 days = _____ weeks _____ days

10) 39 hours = _____ days _____ hours

11) 180 sec = _____ mins

12) 15 days = _____ hours

13) 56 days = _____ weeks

14) 9 hours = _____ mins

15) 170 secs = _____ mins _____ secs

16) 84 days = _____ hours

17) 11 mins = _____ secs

18) 76 hours = _____ days _____ hours

19) 21 days = _____ weeks

20) 660 secs = _____ mins

Score:

Find the perimeter and area of the shapes below, each individual side is 1cm long.

1)

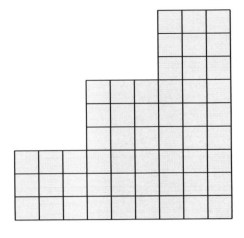

2)

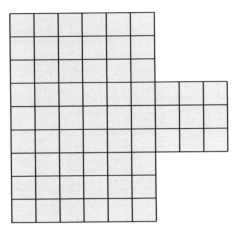

3)

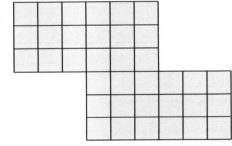

4)

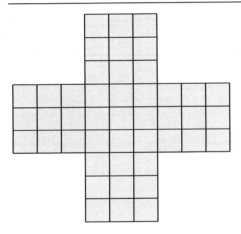

5)

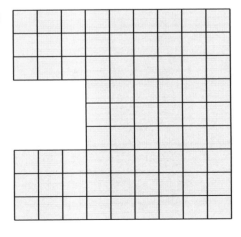

6)

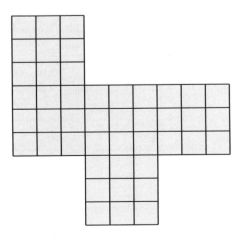

Score:

Estimate the perimeter and area of these irregular shapes.

1)

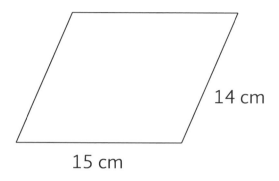

14 cm

15 cm

2)

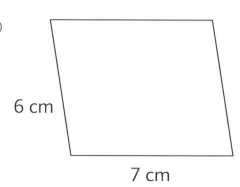

6 cm

7 cm

3)

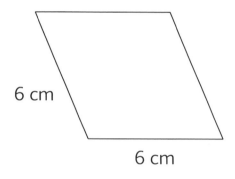

6 cm

6 cm

4)

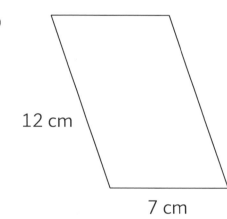

12 cm

7 cm

5)

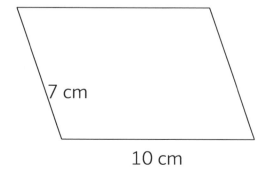

7 cm

10 cm

6)

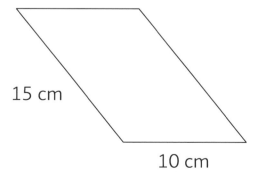

15 cm

10 cm

Score:

Find the volume and surface area.

1)

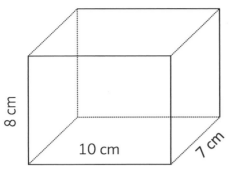

8 cm
10 cm
7 cm

2)

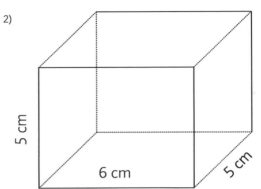

5 cm
6 cm
5 cm

3)

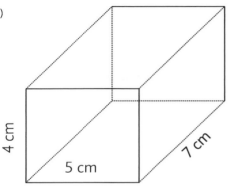

4 cm
5 cm
7 cm

4)

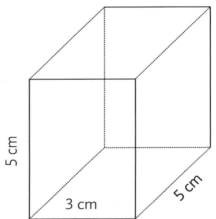

5 cm
3 cm
5 cm

5)

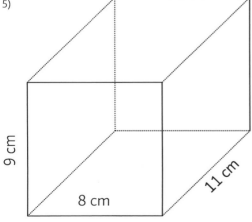

9 cm
8 cm
11 cm

6)

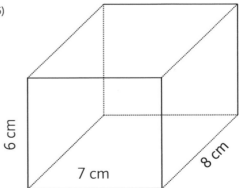

6 cm
7 cm
8 cm

Score:

Write the cubic volume underneath the sets of 3-D shapes below. Each individual cube has sides measuring 1cm. The first one is done for you.

1)
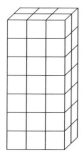

42cm³

2)
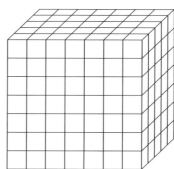

3)
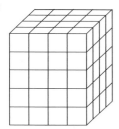

4)
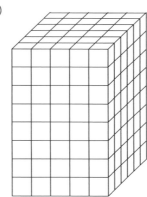

5)
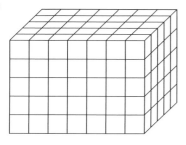

6)
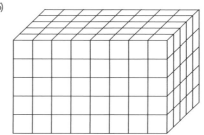

Score:

Identify the polygons.

1)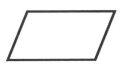

2)

3)

4)

_____

5)

6)

7)

8)

_____

Identify these irregular polygons.

1)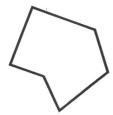

2)

3)

4)

_____

5)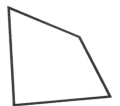

6)

7)

8)

_____

Score:

3-D Polygons

Identify these 3-D polygons and the number of faces for each one.

1)

Name:

Faces:

2)

Name:

Faces:

3)

Name:

Faces:

4)

Name:

Faces:

5)

Name:

Faces:

6)

Name:

Faces:

Score:

Measure and name (acute, obtuse, reflex) the angles. The first has been done.

1)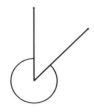

315° - Reflex
_____

2)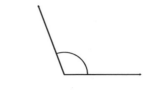
_____

3)
_____

4)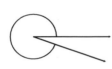
_____

5)
_____

6)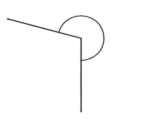
_____

7)
_____

8)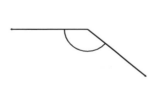
_____

9)
_____

10)
_____

11)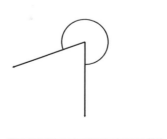
_____

12)
_____

71

Score:

Angles around a point add up to 360°. Without using a protractor, deduct the angle marked out. The first one has been done.

1)

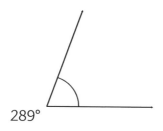

289°

71°

_____

2)

303°

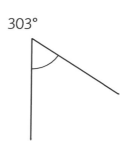

_____

3)

294°

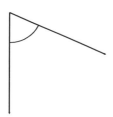

_____

4)

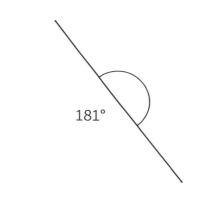

181°

_____

5)

310°

_____

6)

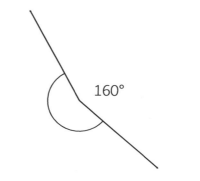

160°

_____

Score:

Solve these time-related angle questions.

1) What is the angle between the hour and minute hand?

_____

2 An hour passes, what is the angle now?

_____

3) Circle the time which has an obtuse angle between the hour and minute hand.

_____

Score:

The shape below is made up of triangles with 60mm sides.

1) What is the perimeter of the whole shape?

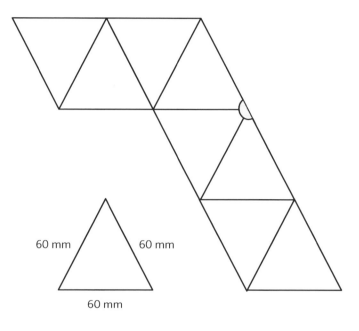

60 mm   60 mm

60 mm

_____

2) What is the size of the angle marked out in grey?

_____

3)) Is there any individual angle that isn't 60°? If not, why not?

_____

Score:

Below is Emily's average scores by month for her Year 5 spelling tests.

Fill out the missing data, adding the x axis, y axis, title and line graph.

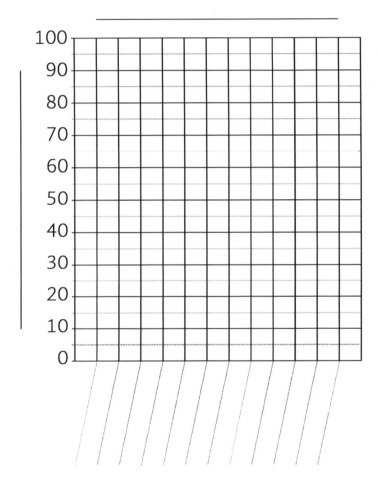

Month	Score
January	50
February	57
March	64
April	68
May	87
June	96
July	98
August	96
September	92
October	88
November	85
December	50

1) In which month did she register her third highest score?

2) Which months did she score the joint lowest?

_____

3) In which months did Emily make a score of over 90?

_____

4) In which months was Emily's score an odd number?

_____

5) Emily's maths scores are exactly half her spelling tests in both June and July. What was the total number of marks she scored in Maths for June and July?

_____

Score:

David is about to catch a train from London and sees the following timetable at the station, some of the information is missing.

Fill out the missing information.

Destination	Departure	Arrival	Duration
Bristol	11:15	12:51	____ Minutes
Leeds	12:47	:	135 Minutes
Manchester	14:25	17:00	____ Minutes
Newcastle	14:40	17:30	____ Minutes
Edinburgh	:	22:22	210 Minutes

1) Which destination had the longest train journey?

2) It is Noon. What is the first train David can catch?

3) Which journey time isn't divisible by five?

4) David arrives at his destination and it is dark outside. Which train did he catch?

5) A first class ticket to Edinburgh costs £80 but a standard fare is nine sixteenths of the first class price. What is the price of a standard ticket?

Score:

Answers

Page 1: Place Value

1. **3 tens**
2. **9 hundreds**
3. **4 ones**
4. **8 thousands**
5. **5 hundreds**
6. **4 ten thousands**
7. **0 thousands**
8. **2 ten thousands**
9. **9 hundred thousands**
10. **9 hundreds**

Page 1: Missing Bricks

1. Subtract 6: **-65, -71, -77, -83, -89**
2. **Add 16: 410, 426, 442, 458, 474**
3. Subtract 6: **-183, -189, -195, -201, 207**

Page 2: Counting on a Line

1.

Page 2: Counting on a Line 2

1.

Page 2: Counting on a Line 3

1.

Page 2: Counting on a Line 4

1.

Page 2: Counting on a Line 5

1.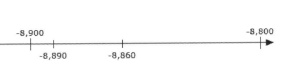

Page 3: Before, After and Between

1. **5059**
2. **-5334 -5332**
3. **-1165**
4. **687**
5. **-9032**
6. **9161**
7. **-3020 -3018**
8. **510 512**
9. **-5712**
10. **-1742**

Page 3: Rounding Numbers

1. **270,000**
2. **200,000**
3. **810,000**
4. **202,240**
5. **667,600**
6. **301,000**
7. **880,480**
8. **588,980**

Page 4: Ordering Numbers

1.		2.		3.		4.	
94.43	8.33	33.65	16.71	43.82	2.07	449	8.79
8.33	62.73	68.19	33.65	2.07	3.35	8.79	25.32
97.96	94.43	594	55.69	5,364	43.82	848.2	68.4
62.73	97.96	16.71	68.19	2,156	2,156	25.32	449
8,917	8,917	55.69	594	3.35	5,364	68.4	848.2

5.
29.4	8.16
11.55	11.55
8.16	29.4
193.3	193.3
7,360	7,360

6.
371	4.41
23.84	5.23
5.23	23.84
2,509	371
4.41	2,509

7.
758	25.85
709	94.2
25.85	578.1
94.2	709
578.1	758

8.
7,164	29.00
869.3	62.6
62.6	869.3
29.00	7,164
7,726	7,726

9.
79.35	1.08
49.8	49.8
797.0	79.35
1.08	477
477	797.0

Page 5:   Circle the Smallest Numbers

1.
(438.50)
795,264
943,525
3,681.95
18,740.9

2.
46,621.8
476,308
(1,059.6)
321,013
4,322.47

3.
53,272.2
6,278.74
(5,414.57)
581,403
7,702.07

4.
62,281
(1,380.51)
91,674
5,900.27
28,179.3

5.
(7,699.07)
864,687
95,026.7
54,010.8
89,497.2

6.
(5,815.07)
685,741
32,897.3
54,486.4
8,150.56

7.
97,301.5
79,182.3
65,235.9
(24,522.7)
987,589

8.
93,757.3
2,790.29
80,850.3
741,247
(1,073.10)

Page 5:   Circle the Largest Numbers

1.
76,319.4
10,141.4
6,252.51
12,371.2
(818,919)

2.
1,857.67
2,888.28
345,693
(683,577)
1,499.0

3.
708,851
6,850.76
(962,538)
95,555.7
172,007

4.
179,162
8,449.96
40,341.7
(473,223)
6,059.01

5.
78,047.7
147,334
(465,732)
50,595.6
459,231

6.
74,089.8
9,755.14
2,962.29
(593,814)
83,263.3

7.
7,832.51
32,954.8
35,042.6
(48,271.7)
5,185.99

8.
668,492
23,943.6
(826,554)
721,188
7,092.04

Page 6: Circle the Smallest and Largest Numbers

1.	2.	3.	4.	5.	6.	7.	8.
(2,404)	(426)	1,821	(3,772)	4,168	(4,567)	3,027	(735)
(401)	728	3,483	1,426	(4,238)	3,194	2,633	(3,253)
874	1,528	(4,615)	(83)	(1,840)	(1,394)	(3,798)	2,343
1,386	(3,738)	(1,104)	88	2,340	3,816	2,588	901
474	2,147	4,437	1,548	3,049	3,669	(1,470)	1,812

Page 6: Negatives: Circle the Smallest and Largest

1.	2.	3.	4.	5.	6.	7.	8.
(-9,155)	-6,860	(-6,151)	-2,398	2,259	(-5,763)	(973)	-2,996
(3,883)	-7,262	-3,325	2,134	1,803	1,865	-7,258	(-2,102)
-3,458	(-9,312)	(-1,680)	(3,760)	(4,240)	-1,427	-4,535	(-8,930)
-2,883	(-1,974)	-4,723	(-6,747)	2,029	(3,163)	-6,708	-8,813
3,614	-8,612	-4,057	-4,452	(-5,907)	-4,068	(-7,832)	-6,227

Page 7: Counting Up and Down 1

1.

-10	0	10	20	30	40	50	60	70	80

Page 7: Counting Up and Down 2

1.

0	100	200	300	400	500	600	700	800	900

Page 7: Counting Up and Down 3

1.

-100	-110	-120	-130	-140	-150	-160	-170	-180	-190

Page 7: Counting Up and Down 4

1.

8,325	8,334	8,343	8,352	8,361	8,370	8,379	8,388	8,397	8,406

Page 7: Counting Table

1.

Count by -15 from 80 to -505

80	65	50	35	20	5	-10	-25	-40	-55
-70	-85	-100	-115	-130	-145	-160	-175	-190	-205
-220	-235	-250	-265	-280	-295	-310	-325	-340	-355
-370	-385	-400	-415	-430	-445	-460	-475	-490	-505

Page 8: Numbers as Words

1. three hundred eleven thousand and eight

2. seven hundred fifty-eight thousand nine hundred and ninety-nine

3. eight hundred ten thousand four hundred and forty-six

4. eighty-eight thousand eight hundred and twenty-four

5. seven hundred ninety thousand one hundred and eighty-eight

Page 8: Words as Numbers

1. 9,267   2. 87,562   3. 33,535   4. 13,543   5. 32,690

81

Page 9: Roman Numerals: Conversions

1. LVIII   2. LIX   3. VIII   4. 49   5. II   6. 9   7. XXXIV   8. 64   9. VI   10. 16

11. 4   12. LXXIV

Page 10: Roman Numerals - Years

1. 1762   2. MDXVIII   3. 1703   4. 1664   5. MMIII   6. 1822   7. 1794

8. 1970   9. MDCXXXIV   10. MDCCCXI   11. 1899   12. 2005   13. 1802   14. MDCLXXV

15. 1702

Page 10: Roman Numerals - Maths

1. XX   2. IV   3. CXVI   4. MMV

Page 11: Input Output

1.
Input	Output
163	335
57	229
131	303
104	276

Add 172

2.
Input	Output
144	168
90	114
179	203
74	98

Add 24

3.
Input	Output
130	246
53	169
32	148
39	155

Add 116

4.
Input	Output
156	350
163	357
76	270
15	209

Add 194

5.
Input	Output
153	176
23	46
156	179
151	174

Add 23

6.
Input	Output
89	203
114	228
189	303
195	309

Add 114

7.
Input	Output
109	110
99	100
133	134
56	57

Add 1

8.
Input	Output
95	285
151	341
115	305
132	322

Add 190

9.
Input	Output
93	267
65	239
184	358
187	361

Add 174

1.

39	+	29	+	74	=	142
+		+		+		+
82	+	14	+	61	=	157
+		+		+		+
73	+	78	+	90	=	241
=		=		=		=
194	+	121	+	225	=	540

Page 12: Across-Downs   2.

92	+	90	+	85	=	267
+		+		+		+
57	+	5	+	61	=	123
+		+		+		+
100	+	86	+	4	=	190
=		=		=		=
249	+	181	+	150	=	580

Page 12:   Table Drill

1.

+	22	14	52	26	97
834	856	848	886	860	931
657	679	671	709	683	754
340	362	354	392	366	437
225	247	239	277	251	322
588	610	602	640	614	685

2.

+	775	550	500	325	19
22	797	572	522	347	41
15	790	565	515	340	34
39	814	589	539	364	58
500	1,275	1,050	1,000	825	519
30	805	580	530	355	49

Page 13:   Addition 0-100

1. 75   2. 99   3. 141   4. 38   5. 161   6. 96   7. 134   8. 154   9. 83   10. 182   11. 147   12. 49

13. 124   14. 144   15. 169   16. 86   17. 95   18. 115   19. 140   20. 98   21. 94   22. 80   23. 75   24. 160

25. 119   26. 115   27. 122   28. 152   29. 139   30. 105

Page 14:   Addition 0-200

1. 136   2. 107   3. 133   4. 58   5. 66   6. 87   7. 148   8. 102   9. 110   10. 94   11. 125   12. 138   13. 101

14. 100   15. 136   16. 168   17. 163   18. 90   19. 168   20. 99   21. 79   22. 117   23. 118   24. 164   25. 143   26. 101

27. 76   28. 147   29. 148   30. 81

Page 15:   Addition 0-500

1. 435   2. 404   3. 469   4. 329   5. 411   6. 467   7. 453   8. 275   9. 231   10. 472   11. 489   12. 415

13. 454   14. 421   15. 369   16. 270   17. 456   18. 425   19. 393   20. 451   21. 327   22. 318   23. 480   24. 458

25. 491   26. 226   27. 433   28. 448   29. 500   30. 215

Page 16:   Addition 0-1000

1. 811   2. 572   3. 753   4. 951   5. 966   6. 812   7. 917   8. 738   9. 918   10. 963   11. 851   12. 884

13. 995   14. 734   15. 981   16. 856   17. 575   18. 893   19. 712   20. 547   21. 883   22. 726   23. 933   24. 713

25. 864   26. 612   27. 592   28. 622   29. 243   30. 786

Page 17:   Addition 0-10000

1. 7,677   2. 4,528   3. 6,079   4. 4,506   5. 5,572   6. 5,690   7. 5,595   8. 5,270   9. 2,465   10. 3,702

11. 3,905   12. 6,900   13. 8,780   14. 7,714   15. 7,372   16. 4,546   17. 5,877   18. 6,155   19. 7,836   20. 4,774

Page 18:   Adding 3 Numbers

1. 100   2. 93   3. 117   4. 93   5. 49   6. 88   7. 106   8. 75   9. 36   10. 59   11. 99   12. 80   13. 73

14. 60   15. 113   16. 28   17. 74   18. 97   19. 92   20. 61

Page 19: Across-Downs

1.

79	–	10	–	46	=	23
–		–		–		–
22	–	3	–	16	=	3
–		–		–		–
20	–	6	–	13	=	1
=		=		=		=
37	–	1	–	17	=	19

2.

94	–	34	–	25	=	35
–		–		–		–
20	–	6	–	12	=	2
–		–		–		–
48	–	20	–	10	=	18
=		=		=		=
26	–	8	–	3	=	15

Page 19: Shade the Correct Answer

1. d) is the correct sum

Page 20: Subtraction 0-100

1. 23　2. 32　3. 70　4. 6　5. 12　6. 7　7. 9　8. 20　9. 47　10. 50　11. 8　12. 14　13. 8　14. 7

15. 38　16. 16　17. 60　18. 10　19. 75　20. 7　21. 21　22. 13　23. 29　24. 36　25. 7　26. 28　27. 23　28. 4

29. 49　30. 36

Page 21: Subtraction 0-200

1. 152　2. 42　3. 3　4. 153　5. 76　6. 3　7. 29　8. 3　9. 106　10. 24　11. 136　12. 25　13. 58

14. 59　15. 2　16. 76　17. 12　18. 18　19. 12　20. 34　21. 14　22. 97　23. 77　24. 5　25. 13　26. 88

27. 56　28. 125　29. 71　30. 95

Page 22: Subtraction 0-500

1. 69　2. 188　3. 157　4. 342　5. 120　6. 51　7. 92　8. 181　9. 186　10. 104　11. 50　12. 306

13. 243　14. 188　15. 342　16. 153　17. 285　18. 174　19. 97　20. 281　21. 115　22. 158　23. 86　24. 149

25. 84　26. 215　27. 71　28. 132　29. 107　30. 136

Page 23: Subtraction 0-1000

1. 231　2. 170　3. 169　4. 333　5. 88　6. 205　7. 86　8. 337　9. 267　10. 140　11. 290　12. 165

13. 123　14. 109　15. 197　16. 448　17. 139　18. 178　19. 95　20. 89　21. 144　22. 296　23. 153　24. 240

25. 126　26. 447　27. 131　28. 282　29. 436　30. 90

Page 24: Subtraction 0-10000

1. 1,024　2. 279　3. 836　4. 229　5. 5,313　6. 2,154　7. 4,589　8. 765　9. 1,132　10. 3,293

11. 2,590　12. 167　13. 2,282　14. 3,272　15. 2,757　16. 2,102　17. 358　18. 4,841　19. 5,261　20. 100

21. 186　22. 2,578　23. 713　24. 255　25. 543

Page 25: Mixed Operations

1. 162　2. 3　3. 12　4. 51　5. 103　6. 20　7. 109　8. 40　9. 130　10. 115　11. 90　12. 16　13. 6

14. 3　15. 125　16. 38　17. 82　18. 26　19. 55　20. 41　21. 24　22. 41　23. 65　24. 71　25. 148　26. 57

27. 38　28. 77　29. 96　30. 95

Page 26: Missing Operators

1. $11 + 14 + 22 + 41 = 88$

2. $18 + 3 + 28 = 49$

3. $2 + 5 - 5 = 2$

4. $2 + 25 + 48 + 14 = 89$

5. $27 + 39 + 8 + 48 = 122$

6. $47 + 1 + 11 = 59$

7. $7 + 37 - 21 = 23$

8. $20 + 35 + 42 = 97$

9. $26 + 39 - 17 = 48$

10. $24 - 22 + 4 = 6$

11. $5 + 1 + 10 + 31 = 47$

12. $16 - 27 - 2 = -13$

13. $14 - 25 - 16 = -27$

14. $12 + 9 + 19 + 49 = 89$

15. $33 + 16 - 18 = 31$

16. $7 + 10 + 13 + 25 = 55$

17. $16 - 4 - 27 = -15$

18. $1 - 21 + 34 = 14$

19. $11 + 3 - 14 = 0$

20. $39 + 31 - 31 = 39$

Page 27: Money Questions

1. £16.48   2. £12.09   3. £149.10   4. £43.38   5. £56.13   6. £180.61   7. £77.65   8. £86.68

9. £111.97   10. £70.89   11. £17.35   12. £185.58   13. £86.27   14. £144.09   15. £64.17

Page 27: Money Word Questions

1. £24.10   2. £252.00   3. £245.00

Page 28: Counting Table 1

1.

Count by -75 from 25 to -3650

25	-50	-125	-200	-275	-350	-425	-500	-575	-650
-725	-800	-875	-950	-1,025	-1,100	-1,175	-1,250	-1,325	-1,400
-1,475	-1,550	-1,625	-1,700	-1,775	-1,850	-1,925	-2,000	-2,075	-2,150
-2,225	-2,300	-2,375	-2,450	-2,525	-2,600	-2,675	-2,750	-2,825	-2,900
-2,975	-3,050	-3,125	-3,200	-3,275	-3,350	-3,425	-3,500	-3,575	-3,650

Page 28: Counting Table 2

1.

Count by 55 from 33 to 2728

33	88	143	198	253	308	363	418	473	528
583	638	693	748	803	858	913	968	1,023	1,078
1,133	1,188	1,243	1,298	1,353	1,408	1,463	1,518	1,573	1,628
1,683	1,738	1,793	1,848	1,903	1,958	2,013	2,068	2,123	2,178
2,233	2,288	2,343	2,398	2,453	2,508	2,563	2,618	2,673	2,728

Page 29: Multiplication 0-12

1. 12   2. 40   3. 28   4. 44   5. 48   6. 18   7. 90   8. 80   9. 108   10. 8   11. 22   12. 40   13. 120

14. 84   15. 32   16. 50   17. 21   18. 0   19. 6   20. 24   21. 3   22. 18   23. 30   24. 121   25. 8   26. 6

27. 12   28. 110   29. 35   30. 63

Page 30: Multiplication Word Problems

1. 10   2. 54   3. 24   4. 45   5. 8

Page 31: Factors

1. 1, 3, 9   2. 1, 5   3. 1, 2, 4, 8   4. 1, 3, 7, 21   5. 1, 5, 7, 35

6. 1   7. 1, 2, 3, 6   8. 1, 17   9. 1, 7   10. 1, 3, 9, 11, 33, 99

Page 31: Venn Diagram: Factors

1. Factors of 75: 1, 3, 5, 15, 25, 75

   Factors of 120: 1, 2, 3, 4, 5, 6, 8, 10, 12, 15, 20, 24, 30, 40, 60, 120

   Common Factors: 1, 3; 5 and 15

2. Factors of 50: 1, 2, 5, 10, 25 and 50

   Factors of 60: 1, 2, 3, 4, 5, 6, 10, 12, 15, 20, 30, 60

   Common Factors: 1, 2, 5 and 10,

Page 32: Multiples

1. 10, 20, 30, 40, 50
2. 13, 26, 39, 52, 65
3. 14, 28, 42, 56, 70
4. 4, 8, 12, 16, 20
5. 7, 14, 21, 28, 35
6. 1, 2, 3, 4, 5
7. 8, 16, 24, 32, 40
8. 2, 4, 6, 8, 10
9. 5, 10, 15, 20, 25
10. 12, 24, 36, 48, 60

Page 32: Venn Diagram: Multiples

1. 12: 12, 24, 36, 48, 60, 72.
2. 15: 15, 30, 45, 60, 75, 90

   6: 6, 12, 18, 24, 30, 36.

   20: 20, 40, 60, 80, 100, 120.

   Common Multiple: 12, 24, 36.

   Common Multiple: 60

Page 33: Prime Numbers

1. 2×2×3×5 (No)
2. 43 (Yes)
3. 2×47 (No)
4. 2×2×19 (No)
5. 5×17 (No)
6. 31 (Yes)
7. 2×2×17 (No)
8. 13 (Yes)
9. 2×3×3 (No)
10. 61 (Yes)
11. 2×3×3×5 (No)
12. 41 (Yes)

Page 33: Prime Numbers

1. 1) 17

   2) 11

   3) 79. (97 is the other option, but it is 8 more than the previous prime - 89)

Page 34: Long Multiplication: Part 1

1. 310
2. 322
3. 312
4. 490
5. 968
6. 330
7. 805
8. 128
9. 189
10. 6,225
11. 335
12. 245
13. 1,624
14. 2,156
15. 2,052
16. 360
17. 3,570
18. 225
19. 5,016
20. 3,256
21. 198
22. 171
23. 1,274
24. 128
25. 0
26. 516
27. 4,875
28. 4,250
29. 1,394
30. 1,547

Page 35: Long Multiplication: Part 2

1. 5,016
2. 26,166
3. 23,206
4. 56,763
5. 1,040
6. 25,489
7. 6,622
8. 15,228
9. 3,696
10. 83,352
11. 2,160
12. 1,720
13. 6,336
14. 3,225
15. 5,612
16. 3,000
17. 784
18. 42,012
19. 390
20. 25,350

Page 36: Long Multiplication: Part 3

1. 79,404
2. 5,505
3. 486,107
4. 323,316
5. 57,848
6. 214,452
7. 513,814
8. 421,806
9. 37,179
10. 303,733
11. 68,985
12. 246,863
13. 18,972
14. 126,434
15. 82,251
16. 426,723
17. 29,046
18. 14,844
19. 28,704
20. 47,880

Page 37: Division 0-12

1. 9
2. 1
3. 9
4. 6
5. 11
6. 8
7. 3
8. 8
9. 10
10. 3
11. 8
12. 11
13. 2
14. 4

15. 3   16. 10   17. 3   18. 3   19. 7   20. 10   21. 4   22. 5   23. 11   24. 9   25. 5   26. 7   27. 6   28. 9

29. 6   30. 4

Page 38: Division Word Problems

1. 9   2. 8   3. 3   4. 8   5. 7

Page 39: Division with Remainders.

1. 22 R4   2. 113 R3   3. 78 R1   4. 84 R3   5. 16 R1   6. 9 R1   7. 61 R0   8. 19 R3   9. 958 R0

10. 105 R0   11. 236 R1   12. 58 R7   13. 478 R1   14. 60 R4   15. 107 R0   16. 82 R1   17. 73 R3   18. 16 R1

19. 47 R2   20. 167 R2   21. 97 R1   22. 42 R2   23. 42 R0   24. 14 R0   25. 42 R2   26. 325 R0   27. 127 R3

28. 64 R7   29. 14 R6   30. 124 R4

Page 40: Division with Remainders: Part 2

1. 1,953 R1   2. 778 R0   3. 863 R4   4. 867 R3   5. 29 R1   6. 227 R4   7. 448 R1   8. 1,179 R1

9. 1,662 R2   10. 1,119 R1   11. 2,345 R2   12. 541 R5   13. 325 R0   14. 883 R0   15. 4,321 R1   16. 751 R2

17. 2,108 R0   18. 216 R4   19. 73 R4   20. 867 R2   21. 1,622 R3   22. 1,568 R3   23. 665 R3   24. 1,721 R1

25. 1,318 R3   26. 155 R1   27. 1,235 R7   28. 606 R1   29. 1,068 R0   30. 1,521 R1

Page 41: Diamond Maths

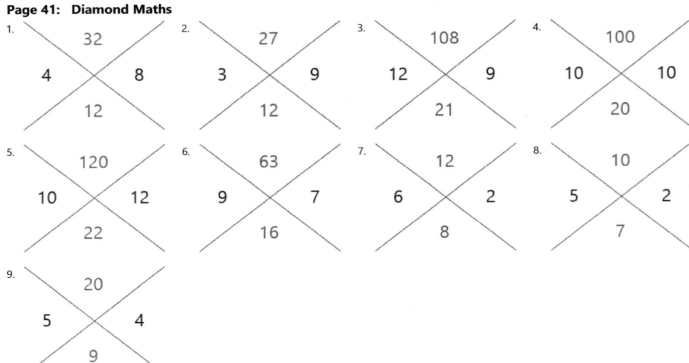

Page 42: Multiplication Boxes

1.

7	1	1	7
10	3	4	120
7	8	8	448
490	24	32	168

21

2.

9	7	4	252
4	8	9	288
6	5	9	270
216	280	324	648

192

3.

6	1	6	36
5	6	3	90
5	9	2	90
150	54	36	72

180

4.

6	4	5	120
2	4	6	48
3	3	6	54
36	48	180	144

60

5.

			36
5	9	9	405
8	1	8	64
4	2	4	32
160	18	288	20

6.

			30
4	3	3	36
7	5	6	210
2	2	8	32
56	30	144	160

Page 43: Powers of Ten

1. 1,500.0 2. 9,900 3. 17,000 4. 1,700.0 5. 21,000 6. 2,100 7. 77.0 8. 7,700.0 9. 48.0
10. 770.0 11. 4.0 12. 6,500.0 13. 55.0 14. 63.0 15. 2,500 16. 860.0 17. 57.0 18. 620
19. 11,000 20. 880.0 21. 72.0 22. 640 23. 44.0 24. 30.0 25. 890.0 26. 60 27. 600.0
28. 75.0 29. 890 30. 590.0

Page 44: Powers of Ten: Division

1. 7.54 2. 37.1 3. 21.4 4. 16.9 5. 7.71 6. 1.87 7. 8.86 8. 98.7 9. 30.6 10. 57.3 11. 6.68
12. 6.9 13. 6.59 14. 15.4 15. 18.6 16. 5.95 17. 47.8 18. 4.24 19. 5.38 20. 41

Page 45: Squared Numbers

1. 4 2. 121 3. 144 4. 100 5. 81 6. 1 7. 25 8. 36 9. 49 10. 9 11. 16 12. 64

Page 45: Cubed Numbers

1. 1,728 2. 8 3. 343 4. 1,331 5. 1,000 6. 125 7. 64 8. 27 9. 1 10. 512 11. 729 12. 216

Page 46: Mixed Operations

1. 24 2. 72 3. 40 4. 11 5. 6 6. 24 7. 18 8. 24 9. 21 10. 5 11. 33 12. 8 13. 4
14. 10 15. 15 16. 4 17. 141 18. 6 19. 86 20. 87 21. 161 22. 5 23. 11 24. 41 25. 142 26. 175
27. 4 28. 160 29. 101 30. 9

Page 47: Identifying Fractions

1. 3/4 2. 3/5 3. 2/6 4. 1/2 5. 6/8 6. 2/3 7. 1/4 8. 3/6 9. 1/3 10. 1/8 11. 4/5 12. 1/6
13. 5/8 14. 1/5 15. 2/8 16. 5/6 17. 2/4 18. 4/6 19. 7/8 20. 2/5

Page 48: Identifying Fractions 2

1. 93/100 2. 12/25 3. 3/50 4. 7/50 5. 63/100 6. 17/20 7. 41/50 8. 13/50 9. 43/50
10. 23/25 11. 69/100 12. 97/100 13. 4/5 14. 1/100 15. 9/20

Page 49: Simplifying Fractions

1. 1/5 2. 2/3 3. 3/4 4. 2/3 5. 2/5 6. 3/4 7. 1/8 8. 1/3 9. 2/5 10. 5/6 11. 2/3 12. 1/4 13. 1/2
14. 1/3 15. 2/3 16. 1/8 17. 2/5 18. 1/3 19. 1/5 20. 7/8 21. 3/4 22. 1/5 23. 1/2 24. 5/8 25. 1/5 26. 1/2
27. 1/3 28. 3/8 29. 1/3 30. 5/6

Page 50: Comparing Fractions 1

1. > 2. < 3. < 4. < 5. > 6. = 7. < 8. < 9. < 10. = 11. > 12. = 13. > 14. > 15. > 16. <
17. > 18. > 19. = 20. >

Page 50: Comparing Fractions 2

1. < 2. < 3. > 4. > 5. < 6. > 7. > 8. < 9. < 10. > 11. < 12. > 13. < 14. = 15. > 16. <

Page 51: Adding Fractions
1. 1/1   2. 13/8   3. 3/5   4. 2/3   5. 2/3   6. 21/20   7. 3/5   8. 7/8   9. 7/6   10. 1/1   11. 3/2

12. 9/8   13. 9/8   14. 7/6   15. 1/1   16. 9/10   17. 3/2   18. 11/8   19. 4/3   20. 11/8

Page 52: Subtracting Fractions
1. 1/5   2. 7/20   3. 1/5   4. 1/10   5. 1/4   6. 1/6   7. 1/2   8. 2/5   9. 2/5   10. 8/15   11. 1/6

12. 1/4   13. 1/15   14. 1/5   15. 1/3   16. 1/8   17. 1/10   18. 8/15   19. 1/20   20. 7/15

Page 53: Converting Fractions
1. 7 1/2   2. 4 1/8   3. 31/5   4. 20/3   5. 5/4   6. 4 1/6   7. 3/2   8. 44/5   9. 43/6   10. 8/5

11. 29/6   12. 6 1/3   13. 29/5   14. 4 3/4   15. 7 2/3   16. 73/8   17. 13/6   18. 4 3/4   19. 49/5   20. 5 1/4

21. 37/4   22. 4 1/4   23. 8 1/2   24. 1 1/2   25. 69/8   26. 34/5   27. 23/4   28. 20/3   29. 7 3/4   30. 4/3

Page 54: Multiplication with Whole Numbers and Fractions
1. 1   2. 4   3. 5   4. 1   5. 2   6. 2   7. 6   8. 3   9. 4   10. 2   11. 2   12. 2   13. 3   14. 4   15. 7   16. 2

17. 4   18. 3   19. 1   20. 4   21. 1   22. 1   23. 3   24. 4   25. 5   26. 3   27. 2   28. 1   29. 2   30. 2

Page 55: Fractions to Decimals
1. 0.6   2. 0.9   3. 0.12   4. 0.65   5. 0.5   6. 0.72   7. 0.2   8. 0.15   9. 0.5   10. 0.1   11. 0.7

12. 0.8   13. 0.5   14. 0.68   15. 0.56   16. 0.48   17. 0.3   18. 0.5   19. 0.62   20. 0.6   21. 0.25   22. 0.9

23. 0.4   24. 0.98   25. 0.33   26. 0.4   27. 0.75   28. 0.48   29. 0.96   30. 0.48

Page 56: Decimals to Fractions
1. 17/20   2. 1/2   3. 11/20   4. 1/5   5. 2/25   6. 13/50   7. 3/5   8. 1/4   9. 4/5

10. 33/50   11. 6/25   12. 8/25   13. 13/25   14. 2/5   15. 9/25   16. 19/25   17. 3/10   18. 22/25

19. 9/10   20. 23/50   21. 37/100   22. 3/20   23. 17/100   24. 1/10   25. 7/10   26. 3/25   27. 19/20

28. 12/25   29. 17/25   30. 43/50

Page 57: Rounding Decimals
1. £69.00   2. £378.80   3. £721.00   4. £478.00   5. £600.00   6. £800.00   7. £970.00   8. £31.00

9. £70.00   10. £170.00   11. £200.00   12. £893.00   13. £496.70   14. £529.30   15. £970.00   16. £840.00

17. £902.00   18. £722.20   19. £350.10   20. £900.00

Page 58: Percentages and Decimals
1. 35%   2. 59%   3. 0.46   4. 0.32   5. 0.8   6. 53%   7. 0.43   8. 62%   9. 64%   10. 0.98   11. 67%

12. 2%   13. 0.63   14. 17%   15. 69%   16. 22%   17. 70%   18. 68%   19. 0.94   20. 0.55   21. 0.25   22. 21%

23. 74%   24. 0.65   25. 0.09   26. 0.75   27. 0.71   28. 0.57   29. 0.11   30. 39%

Page 59: Metric Weights and Measures
1. 0.083   2. 66,000   3. 54,000   4. 33,000   5. 75,000   6. 0.027   7. 88,000   8. 79,000   9. 25,000

10. 22,000   11. 0.023   12. 0.021   13. 58,000   14. 0.022   15. 0.084   16. 63,000   17. 0.072   18. 0.073

19. 0.095   20. 0.071

Page 60: Metric Weights and Measures
1. 0.027   2. 0.046   3. 70,000   4. 0.024   5. 92,000   6. 0.033   7. 0.020   8. 91,000   9. 82,000

10. 96,000

Page 60: Orange Squash

1. 1) 17/18

   2) 2

   3) 589

Page 61: Reading Thermometers

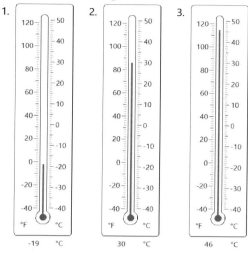

-19   °C   30   °C   46   °C

Page 61: Thermometer Question

1. 65°

Page 62: Reading Thermometers

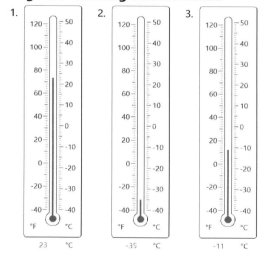

23   °C   -35   °C   -11   °C

Page 62: Thermometer Question

1. Thermometer 1

Page 63: Time Passages

1. What time will it be in 3 hours 33 minutes?

2. What time was it 5 hours 53 minutes ago?

3. What time was it 5 hours 21 minutes ago?

4.

What time was it 5 hours 50 minutes ago?

5.

What time will it be in 3 hours 16 minutes?

6.

What time will it be in 1 hour 50 minutes?

7.

What time was it 3 hours 31 minutes ago?

8.

What time will it be in 3 hours 24 minutes?

Page 64: Time Conversions

1. 3 dy 4 hr
2. 4,800 sec
3. 360 hr
4. 11 wk
5. 1 min 20 sec
6. 2,400 min
7. 1,260 min
8. 720 sec
9. 12 wk 4 dy
10. 1 dy 15 hr
11. 3 min
12. 360 hr
13. 8 wk
14. 540 min
15. 2 min 50 sec
16. 2,016 hr
17. 660 sec
18. 3 dy 4 hr
19. 3 wk
20. 11 min

Page 65: Rectilinear Areas

1. P=36 A=54
2. P=36 A=63
3. P=30 A=36
4. P=36 A=45
5. P=42 A=72
6. P=36 A=45

Page 66: Irregular Areas

1. P=62 A=234
2. P=22 A=30
3. P=20 A=24
4. P=40 A=88
5. P=34 A=70
6. P=56 A=176

Page 67: Volume

1. V=560 cm³ cm³ SA=412 cm² cm²
2. V=150 cm³ cm³ SA=170 cm² cm²
3. V=140 cm³ cm³ SA=166 cm² cm²
4. V=75 cm³ cm³ SA=110 cm² cm²
5. V=792 cm³ cm³ SA=518 cm² cm²
6. V=336 cm³ cm³ SA=292 cm² cm²

Page 68: Volume Cubes

1. 42cm³
2. 245cm³
3. 80cm³
4. 240cm³
5. 175cm³
6. 200cm³

Page 69: Polygons 1

1. Parallelogram
2. Regular Octagon
3. Regular Heptagon
4. Scalene Triangle
5. Square
6. Regular Pentagon
7. Regular Hexagon
8. Rhombus

Page 69: Polygons 2

1. Irregular Hexagon
2. Irregular Heptagon
3. Irregular Decagon
4. Irregular Octagon
5. Irregular Quadrilateral
6. Irregular Nonagon
7. Irregular Pentagon
8. Irregular Heptagon

Page 70: 3-D Polygons

1. 1) Name: Cuboid; Faces: 6
   2) Name: Triangular Prism; Faces: 5
   3) Name: Cube; Faces: 6
   4) Name: Square Based Pyramid; Faces: 5
   5) Name: Cylinder; Faces: 3
   6) Name: Cone; Faces: 2

Page 71: Angles

1. 315° Reflex
2. 110° Obtuse
3. 40° Acute
4. 340° Reflex
5. 345° Reflex
6. 255° Reflex

7. **70° Acute**   8. **140° Obtuse**   9. **65° Acute**   10. **50° Acute**   11. **290° Reflex**   12. **105° Obtuse**

Page 72: Around a Point

1. **71°**   2. **57°**   3. **66°**   4. **179°**   5. **50°**   6. **200°**

Page 73: Angle Word Questions

1. 1) 90°
   2) 120°
   3) Clock 2 - 5:05.

Page 74: Lengths and Areas

1. 1) 600mm/ 60 cms/ 0.6m
   2) 180°
   3) No. All the sides are the same and therefore, all the angles are the same.

Page 75: Emily's Spelling Scores

1.
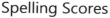
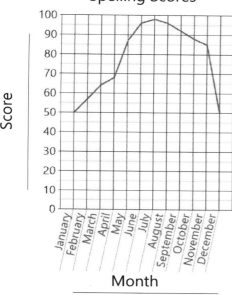

Month	Score
January	50
February	57
March	64
April	68
May	87
June	96
July	98
August	96
September	92
October	88
November	85
December	50

Page 75:

1. 1) September

Page 76: Emily's Spelling Scores

1. 2) January and December

   3) June, July, August and September

   4) February, May, November

   5) 97

Page 77: Timetables

1) Edinburgh

2) The Leeds train

3) Bristol

4) The Edinburgh train.

5) £45

Destination	Departure	Arrival	Duration
Bristol	11:15	12:51	96 Minutes
Leeds	12:47	15:02	135 Minutes
Manchester	14:25	17:00	155 Minutes
Newcastle	14:40	17:30	170 Minutes
Edinburgh	18:52	22:22	210 Minutes

CONTACT: info@junglepublishing.net

Printed in Great Britain
by Amazon